'A beautifully written book spanning continents, decades and cultures'

Dr Amir Khan, author of *The Doctor Will See You Now*, TV celebrity

the red thread

The everlasting invisible connections between us

bina briggs

THE RED THREAD

First published in 2021 by

Panoma Press Ltd
48 St Vincent Drive, St Albans, Herts, AL1 5SJ, UK
info@panomapress.com
www.panomapress.com

Book layout by Neil Coe.

978-1-784529-41-3

To,
Dear Jane, On Mother's Day,
With Best Wishes.
Love and Gratitude.
Thank you for being in my life.

Bina ~~~~ xx

04·03·2022

Dagdusheth Maharaj Ganpati

Dedication

I dedicate this book to our Mummy, Indira.

Young KamalaBaa

KamalaBaa

Mum's sister-in-law no. 5 Kokila	Sister-in-law no. 3 Bhanumati	Mum's Mum KamalaBaa	Sister-in-law no. 2 Neela
Sister no. 4 Lata	Mum's youngest sister no. 5 Anila	My Mum Indira	

KamalaBaa was the matriarch of the family in every way as you can see her personality coming through in all three pictures. The group photo was taken in early 1963 when we had visited India from Uganda, whilst most of Mum's brothers and their families and our grandmother were living in Bihar and West Bengal, in eastern India. Two of Mum's sister-in-laws and two sisters are missing from the picture.

Young Kusum Masi

Sarla Masi

Sarla Masi and Kusum Masi

Kusum Masi was the eldest of the siblings bar one elder brother.
Both Kusum Masi and Sarla Masi were very close. Sarla Masi
was second eldest sister, a wonderful woman who was full of life,
a self-made woman who loved life in every way, a home maker and
an independent soul. She was travelling in a car that was involved in
a serious accident in October 1964. Sarla Masi lost her life, at a very
young age, leaving a young family behind. My uncle was also in the
car and was horrifically injured and unconscious for a long time after
the accident. Our whole family have never got over that tragedy of
losing Sarla Masi at such a very young age.

Testimonials

The Red Thread is a beautifully written book that spans continents, decades and cultures. It tells of the courage and resilience of those who are brave enough to move away from their home countries, but also how by taking traditions and learnings from their birthplaces helps root them to their new homes. Traditional ways of thinking are explored, with a focus on how they continue to be applicable in the here and now. And in the centre of all of this is a very personal story.

Dr Amir Khan MBChB (Honours) MRCGP DCH DRCOG PGCE DipDiab
Honorary senior lecturer, Leeds School of Medicine
Honorary senior lecturer, University of Bradford
Advisory board member, Bradford School of Pharmacy
GP Trainer
GPSI Diabetes
Published author of *The Doctor Will See You Now*
TV celebrity

The Red Thread symbolises the invisible bond of Indian families and communities, the driving force being the mother of the family, our unsung heroes: solid, stoic, protective and beloved. It is the story of the Indian diaspora and their resilience, their warmth and their passion for life. Thank you for making me a part of your journey by even mentioning me in the book. I am humbled and grateful.

Nandini Rawal
CEO Blind People's Association
Treasurer, International Council for Education of People
with Visual Impairment

I'm going to start by stating that I am not the fastest reader of books in the world, I tend to read everything a couple of times and allow the imagination to further create the story in my mind.

With all that said I started and finished your book in a couple of hours, I couldn't put it down and I am being 100% genuine. Knowing you as much as I have come to, I found relating to the book extremely easy, that said I have learnt so much more about you, your family, your views on religion and so much more. With historical links such as changes in Uganda that I simply didn't know in detail apart from just general awareness. I really enjoyed the positivity and optimism displayed throughout your book – it comes through despite adversity. You finish the book thinking WOW that happened – yet feeling happy and positive with maybe more clarity on putting our own lives in perspective! I have many favourites in your book but, being a farmer's boy, the story of your cows milking themselves then ascertaining the reason why and what was found – quite remarkable. I could imagine the scene with the cow hand being amazed and then seeing the shrine developing over the years, loved it! This story and of how you and Ian first met and the diversity you must have had to overcome both family and public. Oh, and the imagery created in the story of how you finally left Uganda, the soldiers, the wait and trepidation of the flight actually taking off... phew...

The book provides a clear feeling of connection and a real understanding of how we can perceive threads of connection in life – sometimes we don't realise they are there and your story provides examples of how they knit together. One last thing, this has clearly been a great creative process and I have enjoyed my read.

Michael Dennis

This book is full of life's lessons, told from the perspective of an Asian woman being brought up in the UK and how merging customs and faiths affected her life. Full of heart-warming stories sharing the overall message that there is love, joy, kindness, hope and gratitude everywhere.

Debbie Gilbert, Viva Business Group CEO, Mums Unlimited Best Business Women Awards

A delightful guide of perseverance, self-growth and resilience. *The Red Thread* is stunningly inspirational and a beautiful guide for those of us who want to continuously grow in life. Bina is an example of overcoming and determination: the energy she transmits is overwhelming! It is very easy to connect with her throughout the reading.

As a matter of fact, every time I thought about the pages I'd read the previous night or the previous morning, I felt so fulfilled, at peace and happy. I felt with the right energy to approach my day from an optimistic perspective. I am so thankful that I have been given the chance to read this beautiful book. I owe to the Briggs family so much in my life!

Pilar Aliaga

My friend Bina has generously let us into her life, and that of her mother, and shown us how it has shaped the wonderful woman I know today. Even if you don't know Bina personally, through this book she shares her life philosophy, and you come away with some of Auntie Bina's wisdom. It's worth it!

Liz Bisson

I am so proud of you for having done this. I am rooting for you and you will always have my love, support and my best wishes. I love you loads and I am so happy we crossed paths when we did.

Ananya Desai

I was truly honoured to be asked to be a test reader for *The Red Thread*. The love shared by Bina and her family is evident throughout the whole book, as is the kindness, compassion and love with which she and her family live their lives. A beautiful book filled with some happy and also some incredibly sad memories but also a deep heart-centred philosophy to live by and to help inspire the reader to live by. A definite must-read for those on a soul-searching journey.

Nidhi Rupa Joshi

The author went through a personal journey to finally find out as a woman that the most important thing is to learn how to, with kindness and gratitude to yourself and others, 'trust the process'. Despite a difficult start in the UK as refugees from Uganda she, her mum and sister focus on the positive side of life.
The Red Thread is reassurance that when we let go, 'everything works out in the end'. It is about acceptance, forgiveness, loving oneself and pursuing your happiness. To me the book is also a reminder that we have to not lose ourselves, be truthful to oneself despite the pressure coming from different directions. *The Red Thread* made me sad and laugh at the same time! I love the author's perseverance in life, stubbornness (she is always right), sticking to her principles and most of all her sense of humour.

Bernadeta Fus

I have loved the love oozing from its pages, the love of your mum, life, family, friends and of course Ian and your business. Lovely reference to Lizzy, you made me smile about our meeting. I was at a book launch increasingly being introduced to some strange people and networking, so yes, on your visit I was initially on my guard but our loved ones brought us together! It's full of your zest and essence.

Jayne Cox
Fusion Spaces Director

My impression is that I feel the book is put together well (it really flows). It came across to me as a book of two halves: the story element and then a teaching element, something like family history meets self-help. What I liked best was the story element. I was totally absorbed by the history, the culture, the religion, the food, the festivals. I was intrigued to learn about the journey that you had been on with your mother and sister. I was inspired by how the three of you handled coming to a new country and settling in, overcoming so much. I was fascinated by your early childhood days, my heart broke when you lost your mother and I laughed at how you knew Ian was the one after sitting next to him that very first day.

Due to enjoying the family history story so much, I found myself skimming the other bits as I was eager to get to more story. I would have been delighted with more story less teaching. Once I got to grips with the format, it was clear. Everything was well described.

Lisa Settle

It was a genuine pleasure reading your book. Thank you. I count myself blessed to have you as my friend, honoured to have been allowed to see your book at this early stage (it made me laugh and cry at various parts, as well as making me think and reminding me of what is important in life). I am humbled to have been mentioned. Related to that, you might like to know that I am currently in Somerset in a 'bubble' with my sister, as she has been furloughed again, and next weekend is the anniversary of our mother's death, so I don't want her to be alone. Just as I was leaving London, on a sudden whim, I decided to bring your mother's beautiful blessed shawl with me, as I needed something precious to give me comfort and strength. You can imagine the warm glow I felt, as I glanced at it, having just read your words about the Freedom ceremony and your generous and thoughtful gift.

The threads that link are complex and wonderful.

I know that your mother would have loved/already loves your book. It is a beautiful tribute to her; so much of you is due to the way she encouraged and inspired you. There is no doubt that she was and would now be even more proud of you.

Kate Griffiths-Lambeth

The Red Thread

The red thread in Hinduism symbolises a sacred bond, commitment, love when two people are tied together, whether that is through a wedding ceremony or between a brother and sister through a *raksha* or *rakhi* or for any special religious ceremonies when a red thread is tied on the right wrist.

For me, it is also the red thread of fate, when people who are destined to meet are tied together with an invisible red thread, which may stretch or tangle but will never break.

Introduction

Dear reader

This book is a series of stories of life lessons, of love, strength, determination, resilience, tenderness, kindness, gratitude, humour, failures, friendships and successes experienced mostly by women. The stories weave mainly through my mum's life, my sister's life and mine, as well as the lives of some of the women whom we have admired. This book spans from the early 20th century to the present day.

However, the message remains the same for the reader. No matter where you are in life, you will come through. Do not despair; there is always a way. Have faith, have a vision to which you are totally committed, believe in yourself and your God, your universe, whoever it is that you believe in. Follow the process. You will be familiar with the phrase, "Ask, believe, receive." Trust the process. It always works out for the better.

Foreword

When I was a child, I used to imagine that each of us trails a thin thread behind us and that our individual strands criss-cross and entwine as we make our way through life. Superficially, this is a book about such connections, but to me it is so much more. It provides a journey full of discovery, a celebration of things that matter, brimming with advice and observations. It is a beautiful tribute to Bina's mother, but, more importantly, it is the story of the life, thoughts and memories that helped to produce that much-loved parent's extraordinary daughter.

I first got to know Bina via social media. We met in real life a year later and I am proud to call her my friend. Despite her protestations, Bina always comes across as interested, calm and caring; this book exemplifies her values and outlook. With beguiling charm, she readily comments on her experiences and offers guidance.

This is an engaging and wonderful book: part autobiography, part philosophy, part tribute to friends, her family and the things that she loves. Honest and moving, it is written from the heart. There is so much wisdom and compassion within its pages. I am sure that you will enjoy it as much as I have.

Kate Griffiths-Lambeth

Contents

Chapter 1

Life is for Living (the Truth is My Life is Good)

The Blessing

This book has been in the making, swirling away in my head for the last ten years, wanting to be out there in black and white, in print. I suppose that some books take a lot longer than that before the writer finally takes pen to paper. I am grateful that at long last it's time to get this out to the world. I am ready.

My life is full of synchronicities, which some would call coincidences. There are no coincidences: things happen when they are meant to happen. One thing I do believe is that things happen for a reason and that they always work out. You will hear me mention this at least a couple of times in this book. So, who am I and why have I this burning desire to write a book?

I am Bina, born as a Hindu Brahmin to a Gujarati family in Entebbe, Uganda. I came to the UK in 1972 with my family when Idi Amin, the president at that time, decided to expel all Asians who had chosen not to take up the Ugandan citizenship. The Asians had been in the country since the early part of the 20th century, mainly because most of the Indian subcontinent was under British rule as were the East African countries of Uganda, Kenya and Tanganyika.

Tanzania as we know it today was formed out of the union of Tanganyika and Zanzibar in 1964, after both had gained independence from the UK. Bar a period of Portuguese domination in the 16th and early 17th centuries, Zanzibar was ruled by the Sultanate of Oman for several centuries until 1822, when it became a British protectorate. It gained independence in 1963 and joined Tanganyika the following year to form Tanzania, but remained semi-autonomous.

We arrived in the UK and were received by a cousin who drove us to Luton, which has been a home since that day.

My mother was born in western India in 1932. At a tender age of 15, she married my father – it was an arranged marriage – and emigrated to Uganda in 1947.

This is mainly our story. The day I agreed to write this book, however, was 30 July 2020, the birthday of a dear friend, Pilar. I remember it so well; it was a life milestone for me and yet, I was full of self-doubts about the purpose and content of the book. I went to bed, still thinking about it all. In the morning, on waking up, I was still feeling these doubts in my head. After my usual breakfast I went up for my bath, still thinking about it all. While in the bath, it suddenly came to me that my purpose for writing this book, and its focus, had been totally wrong. It had to be all about our entwined journeys with lessons learned and most importantly about how we came through it all and for me to tell the tale.

Suddenly, I was grinning away to myself and feeling emotional as I said my morning prayers. The prayers were, as you can imagine, spiritually highly charged, electrifying. I say my prayers every morning because my morning ritual is not completed until then. I have my mum's picture in my *mandir* (temple) at home along with pictures of my favourite deities, including many of Ganesh and some of my dear departed family members, and so I just wanted her blessing. The dear departed are *pitrus* in the Hindu religion and so they are alongside the gods, blessing and looking after us. Therefore, it is totally natural to have them in the *mandir* too.

That morning, I felt as if Mum had given me her blessing. I finished my prayers and went up to my small dressing room to get ready for work, with my mobile in my hand. On my dressing table, there is another picture of Mum. I placed my mobile on the dressing table, in front of Mum's picture, and opened it to look at the theme of my 21-day Deepak Chopra meditation programme for that day. Well, it was no surprise, because it was about "describing your mother and describing positive aspects of her". I just froze at that and looked up, looking straight at my mum's smiling face. The blessing!

I had received her blessing to write the book. That was it, the book was definitely happening. I was smiling, crying, full of emotion, saying, "Thank you." to Mum over and over. Oh, by the way, I talk to Mum all the time. I messaged my husband, Ian, a couple of family members and some close friends. Everyone was just as thrilled as I was, because they knew how much it meant to me.

We all have blessings, though we may not be aware of them, from all sorts of people. We also want blessings from our gods, our elders, parents, anyone whom we hold in high regard. To me, a blessing comes from the heart. A prayer is a blessing; as is every time you think good of someone or tell them to take care, travel safely. I saw a quotation on Facebook that summed up for me what prayers are: a natural feeling of tenderness, love, wishing the person wellbeing, success, prosperity and happiness. The ultimate is to receive the blessing from the one you really want it from. Mum died in October 2003; however, spiritually, she's constantly been with me and my sister and she often makes her presence felt.

You may think that this is utter nonsense; however, to me it is very much part of my life, our lives. I shall be telling you more about it through the book. Therefore, you can see how much it meant to me to have Mum's blessing. After all, the book is about her and me. This book is an anthology in which I'm touching on life lessons, our journey, our characters and the people in our lives who loved us for who we were and what mattered to both of us, and still matter to me.

The Thread

The *rakhi* is a sacred red thread in the Hindu religious tradition that a sister ties on her brother's right wrist, like a bracelet, or a wrist band for their safe keeping and well-being during the festival of *Rakshabandhan*. In return, the brother gives his sister a gift, sometimes of money. In these modern times, the *rakhi* is tied on women's wrists too or, for that matter, anyone whom you want to protect.

So, I always have one tied on my right wrist, blessed by a Hindu priest, or one that would have been adorned by my deities at home in the previous year and which I would have taken off my *mandir* (temple) at home. I often get asked what it is for, I just volunteer the information. I am happy to share information on anything that would be of interest to others.

Mum was a stickler for sending out *rakhis* well in advance to all her brothers and male members of the family in India so that even with the possible vagaries of delayed postal services between the two continents, the *rakhis* would be there before or at least on the day of the *Rakshabandhan*. Somehow, as years went by when in our earlier years in the UK, Mum would write a few lines on the *par avion* flimsy blue writing paper, ask me and my sister to add a few lines too, wrap the rakhis in the letters and seal them in the blue *par avion* envelopes.

As years went by, it became my responsibility to post the letters, under close direction and supervision. The local Indian grocery shop where we bought our *rakhis* – and I still do – would tease us about the number we were going to buy, as it was usually at least 50. Normally a woman would buy a *rakhi* for each of her brothers or/and male cousins, who are counted as brothers too.

She wouldn't have 50 brothers, of course. In Hinduism, a male cousin is classed as your brother and a female cousin as your sister, and all their offspring as your nephews and nieces. Mum liked all the male relations to receive these *rakhis*, so that's how it was, especially as the maternal side of the family extended to third and fourth generations.

It has continued over the years, to this day, and will continue while I'm alive and able to do so. It is my privilege and honour. The brothers have to give me money in return, so it works out pretty well for all concerned. The precious, sacred thread is preserved and continues to bind us as a family. To this day, all my brothers and nephews, who are scattered around the globe, look out for the *rakhis*, as mine are usually the first ones to arrive.

It was a meticulously planned 'operation *rakhis*' this year (August 2020) during the coronavirus pandemic and lockdowns in India and some of the other countries to which I was sending the *rakhis*. The postal service was not up and running in India, so even if I had posted them from the UK, they wouldn't have reached my cousin brothers, so my cousin sisters came to the rescue.

One in Mumbai ordered them from Amazon and got them couriered to everyone in Mumbai and surrounding cities. Another did a similar thing: she sorted out all the ones in Ahmedabad, in Gujarat. The third hub, down south in Bangalore, was taken care of by a lovely niece. The *rakhis* were with the recipients at least two weeks before the festival. Everyone was so happy! Mission accomplished. My sisters and I were not going to let the pandemic stop our brothers and nephews from having their *rakhis*.

I so love my family because of this unity and love we have for one another. It's a massive family as Mum was the eighth of ten siblings: five brothers and five sisters. At one point, there were 125 of us in the extended family. As Indians tend to do, we are all spread across the globe, on four continents. Africa is the only one missing now, but give it time, one of our youngsters will no doubt be there soon enough.

Mum was the only one of the ten siblings who lived outside India and she really missed her family. The letter-writing started soon after Mum emigrated to Uganda in 1947. That was the only way to communicate with the family. Telephone calls were expensive, and telegrams were normally sent to relay bad news, often of a death in the family.

The letter-writing therefore kept her in touch with her beloved family, all meticulously penned in a descriptive style. Mum waited eagerly every week hoping that she would receive at least one letter from her vast family. When one did arrive, Mum used to read it a few times before she wrote her response. The letters took anything from a couple of weeks to a month to reach the recipient, so it was almost a weekly exercise of writing letters to various members of the family. She would often initiate the communication.

Having lived with this kind of bonding, keeping the relationships alive because the family meant so much to Mum, it just came naturally for me to be part of it all. I remember that in the 1970s and 80s, I used to write a lot to all my aunts and uncles, long narratives of life in the UK; I suppose there was a lot to write about at the time. They loved my letters.

One of my uncles, my *masa* (*masa* is uncle, Mum's sister's husband, uncle by marriage; *masi* is Mum's sister, aunt) whom we called Papa, always used to say how much he eagerly waited for my letters as he found them so very detailed and interesting. I would normally write about our personal experiences of anything and everything we encountered in those early years – shopping, transport, people, the seasons, the British weather, the food, what we could get in the way of Indian groceries, including the vegetables, the workplaces, the customs – they were interested in everything. It was easy to describe it all as these were fascinating times for us too.

Life was interesting, as you can imagine; almost everything was a new encounter, learning to lead a normal life with new experiences. Simple things like food. To start with, food did not taste the same as it did in Uganda. Take sugar, for instance: we had granulated cane sugar, which was much sweeter, with very large granules, whereas the beet sugar here in the UK was very bland and almost powdery in comparison. The Indian vegetables were comparatively expensive, so we had them two or three times a week, maximising on potatoes, peas, carrots, cabbage, cauliflower and seasonal vegetables.

There was a vast difference in the meals themselves. Whereas in Uganda and India we were used to having a cooked lunch and a cooked meal for dinner too, in the UK, it was a case of packed lunch at work for Mum and me and a school dinner for my sister. We cooked our one main meal in the evening.

Sadly, most of my aunts and uncles have died and my letter writing has now been replaced by sending WhatsApp messages and greetings cards. I love greetings cards to such a degree that my hubby tells everyone that I alone keep the UK greetings card industry in business.

We are in a different world of communication now. The younger generations in the family engage in digital forms of communication through all the social media platforms, which means that if I want to keep in touch with the youngsters in our family, the third or fourth generation, I have to learn to be in the midst of them, or else I will lose them.

They wouldn't want to write letters or cards to me. They are the generations so far removed that I would become the archetypal aunt who has no idea of who the young relations are, whom I may see once in a blue moon, at a family gathering. I have made it my business to connect with all the youngsters, right down to my great-nephews, great-nieces, great-great-nephews and great-great-nieces on the social media platforms. It's such fun! Love them all so dearly. I learn so much from them, every day, all sorts of things.

The most important aspect of this is that we are staying connected. As I have been handed the baton of letter-writing and maintaining the traditions by Mum, I feel privileged being able to do my bit to keep the thread of communication alive and help the thread of our ancestry to continue.

Love and Gratitude

We all know love in its many forms. We all love others, just as much as others love us. We crave love, we celebrate love, we love to love and yet at times love can be so painful. There are hundreds of definitions of love, subjective as well as objective. Love in its purest sense does not expect anything in return. The meaning of love has been defined in every scripture of every religion to the nth degree.

I'm neither a scholar nor a philosopher so what do I know of love? Simply put, for me, it means love for my husband, my parents, siblings, family, my friends, my cats, my career, my business, nature, the human race and anything that creates a feeling of affection. Each to me is a different kind of love, but it's still love. The love that brings me happiness, joy, a warm feeling of life with a meaning for my existence.

However, love can hurt us too, causing a lifetime of pain and misery. Unrequited love is such that it tears our lives into shreds, a dark existence with no hope of ever coming through to the other side. Mum experienced that for over 25 years when her love wasn't reciprocated. She endured every kind of atrocity and abuse that only a woman can relate to. Married life started well; however, within five years of the marriage, it went terribly wrong.

Mum had no escape, so she endured it over and over, every day, without letting anyone know. Then, as I grew up and started to see, feel and understand the situation, I knew what it was like to have a dominant, dark, overwhelming personality in our lives. The outside world had no idea what was going on; isn't that often the case? Fortunately, we came through it, lived our lives away from that existence. It came with Mum's determination, resilience and our destinies taking us on a separate path from my father's.

A strange thing happened while I have been writing this chapter today. I looked at my mobile and Siri was showing me a blog I had written for a series called Advent Blogs on Twitter in 2013, titled, 'For the Love of You'. Mother's love! Serendipity, as a friend said when I told her about it. I know that Mum just sent me this message to let me know that she's here with me.

The blog was all about my mum's journey to the UK, her love for her daughters and family, the people who came into her life, neighbours, work colleagues and from any community in Luton, how she took them under her wing. It also highlighted how a mother's love through centuries has depicted selflessness, love in its purest form.

Gratitude was a word that was always there in my dictionary, but consciously, was I actually grateful? Have I always been grateful for what I am, who I am and where I am in life? I can truly say that it did not register with me until later in life, when looking back; I realised how lucky I am and have been.

For me as a Hindu, gratitude is one of the pillars of being a good human being but the sudden dawning of an all-embracing, all-knowing feeling of awakening in every cell of my body to feel that feeling of gratitude is something else. Yes, I've gone through life thinking, "Why me?" as most of us do from time to time, some more than others and for some, for a lifetime or for long periods in their lives. Fortunately, I woke up from that a very long time ago. These are all life lessons and gratitude came to me in a way that it has become very much who I am. You could say that I have been reborn.

It all started with me having to suddenly leave a much-loved job as head of human resources at the airport. Suffice to say that although on the outside I was being very professional, inside I was crying and grieving. I was shell-shocked. I couldn't go back into another high-level corporate job and so became a partner in an HR consultancy, Plain Talking HR. During my initial years in the business, I came across an HR community on Twitter like no other, who welcomed me with open arms.

I'm very much part of it now and so grateful. One day someone started using the **#3goodthings** hashtag and the psychology behind it. It took me a while to understand it or even to try it for myself. I found out that this lovely HR contact was running a session for any of us who were interested to learn a bit more about it. I registered my interest to attend.

Soon I was on a lovely training course in London for a three-hour session, which left me wanting to know more. After the session, we all strolled down the street, bought our takeaway lunches from a nearby deli and there we were, some 15 of us, on a warm sunny afternoon in Regent's Park, sitting on our bit of grass, having a picnic. We were all chatting, laughing, taking in the greenery around us. I was thinking, "Wow, I'm in the middle of London, having an impromptu picnic with people I don't really know," and yet felt so comfortable with them, with the whole scenario. It was nothing I had imagined it to be like that day when hey presto, Gratitude made a grand entrance into my life. I wasn't sure about it; I did not understand it enough (I'm not a psychologist either) but it felt right.

I wanted to give it a go. In the beginning, it was a struggle to find **#3GoodThings** that had happened to me every day that I was grateful for. I stuck to it, determined that I was going to make it work. The best thing that happened with this process was that I don't remember when I stopped counting because I was filling up the diary page each night with all the good things that had happened on that day. That lovely HR professional who delivered this free course knows this as I have mentioned it to him a few times in the last few years.

Living

"My mission in life is not merely to survive, but to thrive and to do so with passion, some compassion, some humour and some style." Maya Angelou could have said this about any of us. This was definitely my mum. It feels so right as a principle to live by. It is for all women; like Maya Angelou, my mum and you and I in some way as women have strived for our right to live our lives to the fullest.

Mum's passion was her zest to live, to experience new life events, travelling, new foods. Mum loved variety in everything. Often after a couple of days of eating the usual Gujarati staple food of *rotli, daal, bhat* and *shaak*, she'd say, "I want to eat something different, something tasty but I don't know what." We'd then go through menu options and end up with something tasty or a derivation of the initial menu, such as *vaghareli rotli*, meaning tempered *rotlis*. Most Gujarati households always make some surplus food every mealtime, especially the staple items such as the four I mentioned earlier.

The leftovers are either warmed up and eaten along with the fresh dinner items or used as base ingredients to make another dish. This is creative cooking at its best. So, we'd make fried rice or the *vaghareli rotli*, by mixing the leftover rice with the *rotlis*, shredded into small pieces, tempered with all the spices, along with garlic, onion, green chillies, green coriander in a yogurt sauce. All very tasty. It didn't matter what it was, it had to be piping hot, the plate or bowl heated up in the oven to keep the food warm.

As for the compassion, I can never match her compassion for all creatures great and small. Even when she was not that comfortable with my cats around her, she always showed compassion, especially as they all made a beeline for her and wanted to cuddle up to her while she was sitting on the sofa, reading or knitting. Mum spoke to all of them in Gujarati and it seemed to work very well!

I also remember the time in Uganda when my sister was quite young and my father bought a puppy from someone he knew. The poor puppy cried all day and all night. At night it was so pitiful. Mum stayed up all night trying to calm it, singing lullabies to it, cuddling it. The poor puppy was missing its mum. After about five nights of the same thing, Mum asked my father to take the puppy back to the owner who still had the puppy's mum.

Mum had a wicked sense of humour, which I feel that I have inherited. At times, it starts bubbling up at the most inappropriate times. I remember a time, soon after I was married and Mum was staying with us, when a late-night film was being shown on TV, a teenage cult film, *Porky's*. Funny but risqué, it was about a young guy's friends helping him to lose his virginity. Not the kind of movie one would want to watch with Mum, but Ian, my husband, said, "It'll be fine." Well, Mum couldn't stop laughing, all the way through, often with tears running down her cheeks. I can still see her collapsing with laughter.

As for style, Mum had a great sense of dressing and colours. She loved bright colours and I have definitely inherited that from her: the brighter the better. I used to love the colour blue when I was a teenager and in my early 20s. Mum got fed up with me always buying clothes in blue, so she told me to buy any colour other than blue when I went shopping for clothes. She would say, "Don't come back with blue, buy any other colour."

Well, somehow, I cannot really wear the colour blue now. It just doesn't do anything for me anymore. Give me the reds, oranges, fuchsia pink, green, gold, yellow and even white, cream or black, anything but blue. Life is colourful, so why restrict myself to a couple of colours, eh?

I am a firm believer in life lessons and living life to the fullest in the way I can. So, I still have lots of ambitions and dreams to fulfil, such as seeing and being in one of the hot air balloons at the Albuquerque International Balloon Fiesta and of course flying a kite at some of the big kite-flying festivals of the world.

To me, age is just a number, so there is still much to experience. Both hubby and I feel the same about it. The soul never grows old, even though as the years go by there is more of a stranger looking back at me when I look in the mirror. Eeeeeek: that's all I have to say on that subject.

Living is all about grabbing every moment we can and living it as well as we can. Both Ian and I have lived with that motto. It's been a good life; a lot of it has been a surprise to say the least, often fantastic, sometimes a bit meh.

In the main, it has been a great life with so many wonderful experiences that I would have never thought of in my wildest dreams, including running a business; or being in the press facilities at the 24 Hours of Le Mans over a number of years with Ian while he was writing a book on sports car endurance racing; or being in the state forests of Pennsylvania while Ian was riding in a long-distance cyclo-cross race; or visiting the sites of the American Civil War – including Gettysburg and the seated statue of 'Honest Abe' (Abraham Lincoln) at the Gettysburg Museum and Visitor Center nearby.

The point here is that we are always looking forward to life. Life is for living and my message for you is that the human spirit is unbreakable. We all have a choice to live a better life today than yesterday, and tomorrow will be just as good as today, if not better.

Chapter 2

It is YOUR Life to Celebrate Every Day (No Matter How Hard it May Be)

Faith and Festivals

Diwali and New Year

Life is for celebrating, for all the small wins we have every day as well as all the bigger ones in life, whether they are based on family, traditional, religious, national or global events. Celebrations not only give us reasons to acknowledge these wins, but they also strengthen our faith and restore hope for the future. Each day is a new dawn to be celebrated. No matter what life throws at you, find something in that day to celebrate. During the dark times of our life in Kampala, there were festivals too, time to celebrate and forget your troubles for a while. Faith has always played a big part in our family, in our lives, in my life.

For me, Hindu religious festivals are a way of life. I probably don't celebrate them in as passionate a way as I used to when Mum was alive.

Since coming over to the UK, a lot of things have changed. Life in Uganda was very different. People of my mum's and dad's generation, born in the early 1920s and 1930s, preserved the traditional Gujarati way of life that they had known in India. They took the traditions, values, strict vegetarian food, religious fasting and festivals with them. Religion played a great part in it all. As India and the East African countries of Uganda and Kenya belonged to the British Empire, the Asians were given British passports to emigrate to the East African countries to build the railways, roads, industries and pretty much everything as part of development of those countries.

Diwali is the last day of the year in the Gujarati calendar when in the Hindu scripture of Ramayana, Lord Rama returned to his kingdom of Ayodhya after spending 14 years in exile. Diwali means festival of lights; the road to Ayodhya was lit for Lord Rama when he returned to his kingdom. Thus, on Diwali, *divas* (lights) are lit inside and outside the houses, usually made of earthenware holders with oil in them and a wick made of cotton wool. These days, there seem to be permanent outdoor lighting displays in and around the home.

The Diwali festival is celebrated over almost a fortnight, starting in the last week of the year and going beyond Diwali to New Year's Day and the second day of the new year, which is called *Bhai Beej* or *Bhai Dooj*, Brother's Day, when sisters invite their brothers for lunch at their homes. Every festival has a meaning and a different celebration, along with different food. A bit like Christmas and New Year celebrations, only it lasts a lot longer.

My early childhood recollections of Diwali celebrations in Kampala are of making and eating lots of different varieties of vegetarian Gujarati food, listening to lots of Indian film music of our favourite singers – Lata Mangeshkar, Mohammed Rafi, Hemant Kumar, Mukesh, Manna Dey, and Asha Bhosle, to name a few – along with music from favourite films of the time. It was also an opportunity to wear new clothes every day of the festivities, and to be with your loved ones, family and friends. It was the one time that fireworks were the cherry on the top; I always managed to get a hand or a foot burnt by a fire cracker. It became a family joke that unless I was burned at least once during the festive period, Diwali hadn't come to our household. The Gujarati and the Hindu communities celebrated Diwali in style.

In Kampala, the food was made in huge quantities, for all the mealtimes, especially for lunch every day with a different menu. It was a case of food glorious food in abundance with a menu made of our favourite desserts, which were eaten with the main meal, made out of milk, yogurts, wheat and chickpea flours.

The milk-based sweets, such as *doodhpak* or *kheer* (rice puddings) or the yogurt one called *shrikhand,* usually did not contain ghee (purified butter) – but the flour-based ones did.

Then there were the different vegetables and lentils cooked in various ways too. In addition, there were the savoury snacks like *mathias, chevdo* – 'Bombay mix' as it's known now in the UK; which were a must, always made for Diwali – and *ghooghras* (rattles), little semolina-filled sweet parcels in plain flour pastry, deep fried with lots of sugar, nuts and spices in the semolina filling. These were the main items that were essential for Diwali, along with lots of other foods, snacks that are not normally made regularly, all full of ghee and sugar if they are sweet and fried if they are savoury, called *farsan.* We all loved Indian sweets made with ghee, I still do.

Everything was home-made from scratch. I remember even pounding grain or milling flour as a normal part of our food preparation. My mum was an excellent cook, and had learned from my eldest paternal aunt, Dad's brother's wife. All the women of the neighbourhood got together in that last month of the year and cooked in turn for the different households.

All the kids helped, especially the girls. So, we became the *toto jikoni,* Swahili for 'kitchen kids' meaning kitchen assistants or kitchen help. I learned cooking at an early age, and was able to cook a full Gujarati staple meal of *daal, shaak* (green vegetable), *bhaat* (rice), *rotli* (roti) by the age of 9 or 10.

Another well-loved tradition was of the Gujarati New Year's Day when everyone wore new clothes. Mum was a wonderful dressmaker, making dresses for me, my sister and cousins, and her own sari blouses. This was always a last-minute race to get it all done before the Diwali night.

On New Year's Day, it was a tradition that everyone went to the temple for prayers and then to one another's houses, wishing everyone *Saal Mubarak* (a happy new year), which may seem like a non-Hindi word, but it just means felicitations of the new year. There is a pure greeting of *Nutan Varshabhinandan* which means the same, but is reserved as a formal written greeting.

We woke up very early that day and were ready by 6am, with our new clothes on, the house all cleaned and welcoming, lunch already made or most of it ready. The snacks were ready, served in compartmentalised dishes, to welcome the visitors as they arrived to wish us happy new year. The doorway was always decorated with garlands of flowers or with a *rangoli* on the floor, and just outside the front door, a *mandala* of dry coloured powders.

We then waited for family, friends and neighbours to come over to wish *Saal Mubarak*. We reciprocated by going around to their homes. This was also the occasion when you would bow to your elders for their blessings. Often the elders would give gifts to the children and younger family members with the blessing.

These traditions came with us to the UK and in some parts of the country, such as in Wembley and Leicester where there are huge Gujarati and other Hindu communities, they are very much alive and flourishing. In my town, we all visit the Luton temple for these festivities, especially on New Year's Day for the 10.30am prayers and *aarti*, followed by a 1pm lunch darshan of the *Annakut*, the feast for Lord Krishna, limitless food. This is when the community members bring a food item of their choice: sweet, sour, spicy, fruit, it could be anything as an offering to the gods. These are all arranged in front of the deities and then shared out to the community after the evening prayers. There are typically at least a hundred varieties, all beautifully displayed. This is also the time of meeting and greeting fellow community members at the temple, an occasion of happiness.

Dagdusheth Maharaj Ganpati

Siddhivinyak Ganpati

Ingorada Hanuman

Ganesh and Hanuman

There are so many other religious festivals that we all love; however, there are two other festivals that I love, one of Ganesh and another one of Hanuman. The Hindus have thousands of deities who are worshipped with the same reverence and faith; however, we all tend to have our own favourite god or gods. Mine are Ganesh and Hanuman.

Ganesh is always worshipped first at the beginning of any religious prayer or ceremony, service. I love Ganesh and so I just fall in love every time I see a *murti* (statue or ornament) depicting Ganesh, a bit of an obsession really to be honest. Family and friends therefore seem to gift me Ganesh ornaments, artefacts and statues quite a lot. I'm so happy to share my love of Ganesh with anyone who is interested in him that it feels natural to buy a gift of a Ganesh *murti* for them.

As for Hanuman, well, there's a beautiful story dear to my maternal family. Mum's great-grandfather, who lived in our ancestral village Halvad in Gujarat state nearly 200 years ago, was fairly well off and owned quite a few cows, which he farmed for milk and dairy products. He employed a cowherd who would take the cows out of the village to pastures for grazing, returning the cattle in the evening to the family home, where my great-grandmother would milk all the cows, except for one that never had milk to give.

This happened over a long period so Great Grandma challenged the cowherd about it, saying he was stealing the milk. The poor guy said he had no idea of what he was being accused of, so he started watching this one cow very closely on the way home every evening. He found that at the outskirts of the village, the cow would walk away from the herd and stand on a hillock, where all the milk from her udders would run out. This happened every evening; she always stopped at the same place.

The cowherd asked our great-grandfather to accompany him over a few evenings to witness this phenomenon and true to the cowherd's story, it happened every evening. Great Grandpa consulted the village elders, who advised him to have that spot dug up. This was done and, to everyone's astonishment, a huge stone statue of Hanuman was found underneath.

Our great-grandfather had a small shrine built on that spot and the deity consecrated. Over the years and generations, that deity has become Mum's family Hanuman at Ingorada. We all have absolute faith in him. We love him totally. The family members, old and young, visit the temple frequently, especially for life events, occasions, or when someone wants a special blessing, or just to pay their respects. What is so heartening over the decades is that our younger generations are just as much in love with him as we oldies are.

The small shrine has now become a large temple with lots of other facilities, all sponsored and maintained by Mum's brothers when they were alive and now by my cousin brothers and their offspring, and so it will continue with the future generations. In January 2019, the family had a plaque put up with our family name and the history of the temple in brief; we were all so moved by it and so proud of that day.

I was fortunate to be there at the time, with a number of elders, cousins and their other halves. We all piled on to a big bus and visited the temple from Ahmedabad and made a great day out of it. There were around 40 of us, young and old, and we all enjoyed the visit, then went on to our village and the family's favourite Lord Shiva temple, where lunch had been arranged. The lunch was a full celebration, typical of our village lunch with the laddoos. On the way home, we played music and games and the singing was in full flow – no volume control.

Every time Mum visited India, or when I have in recent years, we always managed to get to the Hanuman temple to pay our respects. I try to get out to India at least once a year in January, in their winter; it is a pilgrimage in its most simple form.

At the local Hindu temple in Luton, the festival of Hanuman's birthday has been celebrated with prayers over a number of years. Each time, the Hanuman prayer of 40 verses, *Hanuman Chalisa*, is recited 108 times. I have been known to sit in one place on the floor, cross-legged for 11 hours, to complete the 108 prayers. Hanuman is known for his strength and I know that he's always given me the strength to see me though these prayer sessions and much more, every time I have asked him.

Christmas

Well, you probably didn't expect to see Christmas on here as one of my favourite festivals. We knew about Christmas in Uganda, as it was a British colony until 1960 and is a Christian country; however, as Hindus, we did not celebrate it in our family. That all changed when we arrived in the UK in October 1972; Christmas was just around the corner.

Within five weeks of our arrival in the UK, I found a job working for Court Line Aviation at the local airport as a junior admin and data clerk. Christmas preparations were in full swing in the company and in my department. My colleagues took me under their wing and there I was, going to my very first Christmas lunch of nut roast, which was mashed potato with a few almonds, accompanied by boiled potatoes, chips and Christmas veggies as the vegetarian option. I didn't mind it at all.

Christmas was all around us and so we got swept along with the euphoria of all things Christmas, including having a small tinsel tree in our rented two rooms, small gifts for the three of us. It was all very new to us, being able to buy gifts for one another in the way that we did, the decorations, Christmas food and cards for friends and family.

Over the passing years, Christmas has become part of our family festivals. We all love it, and Mum loved it just as much. While Mum was alive, it was a family affair through the festive period; we were in our element. Mum used to always make a new outfit for herself for Christmas Day. It often would have red in it because all festivals are auspicious and therefore the colour red, being an auspicious colour, featured in her outfit. Mum always bought a bottle of good whisky each for her two sons-in-law – well, I did, and wrapped them up for her to give out on Christmas Day.

To this day, that tradition is well and truly alive, in the name of absent friends. As a Hindu, with a Christian hubby, I am more passionate about it than him. God is God, no matter in what form one worships God. It's all about God, love, faith, family, friends, gratitude for our good fortunes, giving, receiving and enjoying life, celebrating it. What more can one ask for?

Mindset

I thought a lot about mindset before writing about it. How one thinks or approaches life is the context in which I'm writing about it. I had never thought too deeply about it until I realised that the way I train my mind and the way I approach life, no matter what is happening to me at that precise time, affects the outcome; it has been in my hands.

Mum had a tough mindset. Determined to stand on her own feet, she would tackle the elements, even though it was snowing and slippery and she had rheumatism in both knees; she would get on the bus every morning at 6.30am to be at work before 8.00am, ready to start. She took a job in a garment factory when she was a trained teacher, just so she could earn a living for all three of us. The bonds she made there lasted to some extent until now. Even after being made redundant she did not lose the independent mindset that she instilled in us.

We talk about people having a fixed mindset when they have a certain attitude towards everything they come across; feel they must solve every problem, otherwise they look silly or stupid. Then there are others who feel that one's mindset is flexible; you can develop it in life to have certain attitudes and skills, which can be taught.

I know that I'm stubborn and often have a fixed mindset, but I'm often very happy to take on board what I'm being taught, being flexible in my thought processes. Flexibility is the key for me and it works every time.

You may think I'm talking total rubbish here. However, I can only tell you how I have come out of some really dark periods in my life. Instead of looking at the whole day as one dark solid period, I started looking at little rays of light through the day. I expected things to work out, to have solutions present themselves to me.

I opened my mind to new ideas and not saying, "No," as the first impulse or reaction, especially when meeting new people at networking, or in meetings where perhaps things are being said that I may not agree with. I do persevere with listening and thinking it through, rather than jumping in with my first reaction. It has taken a lot of effort, mindfulness and cultivating good habits, such as meditation and changing the negative vibes to positive ones. I set myself up now to succeed where once I had a fear of failure. I have reformatted my thoughts and it'll be an ever-evolving lifetime process for me. Meditation, kindness, giving and forgiving – to name a few aspects of this – have helped me.

Forgiveness

When one has experienced trauma, tragedy, hardship, scarcity, physical or mental abuse in one's life, the mind decides how it wants to see the world around it. Often it is not that easy for one to get out of victim mode, especially if one sees a downward spiral and everything seems to be stacked against one.

Mum had all this thrown at her and more. She had her dark moments when there seemed to be no way out of it. Fortunately, that changed for the better. In the early years of separation from my father when we remained in the UK and he moved to India, forgiveness was not something Mum or I were good at, not for my father. A very long time after that, decades later, all that changed too.

I had wanted to visit a psychic after Mum died, but it took another seven years before I did so. In the first few years, I was totally shattered by my loss, which I had never thought would affect me in the way it did. I kept thinking of how I wanted to know how Mum was in the spiritual world. I couldn't summon enough courage to do so. I wanted to know and at the same time, I didn't know how I'd handle it. I kept looking for someone I felt I could trust, someone who may come with a recommendation.

A dear friend gave me the contact details of a psychic. I went to meet this lovely old lady at her little bungalow in Biggleswade who just wanted to know the month of my birth. She didn't ask my name or anything else. Praying that Mum would come through, well, Mum and my father both did, together.

I expected the psychic to say that Mum was there, but she said that my father was there too, that he had died over 20 years earlier. I was just shocked. Mum said a few things, but then my father started telling me things that no one else knew or would have ever known at all. He asked for forgiveness for what he had done to our lives.

I was so numb and overwhelmed, I started sobbing my heart out. Even after the reading, driving home more than 20 miles, I couldn't stop crying. On arriving home, I wrote out pages of notes of everything I remembered of the reading, what both had said to me. They were together and loved each other, as they always had in the beginning. Oh my God! Forgiveness is something that doesn't come easy to most of us. It took me a long time before I forgave my father. I have made my peace with him now.

Kindness

This experience has taught me to be kind. My Mum was a kind person, with a heart of gold. I try to live up to those qualities of kindness and generosity, for myself and others. Mum had the knack of connecting with everyone. She was benevolent to a fault. If someone needed something, she was there with it. She was no one's fool either, so she didn't get taken in by flattery or flummery. A very straight-talking woman who did not find it difficult to speak her mind when it was required. I have been told at least a couple of times that I am like Mum in that respect; a bit of a surprise or not, eh?

As a human being, especially in a society where we are told from childhood to think of others first, be kind to others, be generous to others first, it becomes very difficult to train oneself to do anything else. To think of oneself first, to be kind and take care of oneself. In the last decade or so, people have become much more aware of self-care when the law of attraction, yoga, the meaning of life, gratitude and kindness, thinking of oneself are all very topical.

What does it mean to be kind anyway? I'm sure there are several definitions in different contexts. However, for me, simply put, being kind means being a human being, treating others as I would like to be treated. Making it personal to be benevolent, considerate or just giving that individual a little extra attention. We all love personal attention, something that touches our hearts, a small gesture of consideration, being seen as an individual. Have you noticed that most of the time, you feel it in your heart and so the action is flawless, a reflex action; it feels right in that moment?

Recently, I had ordered some exquisite gifts for friends, Christmas presents. The young lady from whom I had ordered these decided to travel from Leicester to Luton to deliver them personally. I thought the gifts were being delivered by courier when I received a message to say that she was coming down with her husband in the next couple of hours. I just bought her a small bouquet of flowers to thank her for her trouble, but the big smile on her face said it all. She later put it on her Instagram to say how kind a gesture it had been.

Giving

Kindness flows into giving, whether that is your attention, your time or some other gift. The more one gives, the more it's returned to one, says the law of attraction. Giving when you don't have that much to give is what it's all about; when it is given from the heart, it binds the giver and the receiver in an invisible unique bond.

One of my fond memories of Mum was of her forever knitting and sewing baby clothes as soon as she knew that someone – in our family, circle of friends or in the wider community – was expecting a baby. Everyone loved these gifts, as they were always of the highest quality and taste, made with love.

Charity begins at home, as the saying goes. However, it is still very much a new concept for a lot of us when you are used to giving to your family, community, wider neighbourhood and your country, and then you are reminded that you should give yourself the same kindness and consideration.

Until much later in life, Mum didn't have that much in terms of wealth to give, but it never stopped her. This is how she showed her love and gratitude. Every time she visited India, from 1973 to 2001, the Indian tradition of giving gifts was very much at the heart of it. Suitcases full of chocolates and carefully chosen gift items were packed, enough for every member of the extended family.

We made several shopping trips to the town centre in Luton to buy these items, or even to Wembley to buy the easy-wash-and-dry Japanese-printed saris that couldn't be bought in India. A bit like taking coals to Newcastle, I know, but they were appreciated all the same for the fine materials and quality of printing. This was also the time of overweight bags, heavy bags that had to be carried by someone. It was always a game of wits to see how much extra luggage could be taken without paying for it at the airport. Mum somehow always managed to get a lot through without paying any money for it at the check-in desk.

A lovely story comes to mind. On one of these trips, Mum was waiting in the baggage reclaim area at Mumbai Airport, looking out for her bags. She saw them on the carousel coming towards her, so she asked a young man standing next to her if he would be kind enough to help her to get them off the carousel. The young man smiled and said, "No problem." Mum was being met by one of my cousin brothers and his son at the airport, and as they met Mum outside the arrivals hall, there was a crowd of people and a bit of a commotion around a person nearby. Suddenly the nephew got excited, pointing to the person in this crowd, saying the name of a famous Indian Bollywood actor: Rishi Kapoor. Mum looked and said, "Oh that's the nice young guy who helped me with my bags."

Mum loved knitting and once she knitted Aran wool hats for all my uncles (her brothers) so that they could wear them in the Indian winter months. Although not worth that much, to the brothers, these gifts were invaluable. The fact that she had thoughtfully knitted these hats for them, we could see the sheer love and pleasure in their eyes; it was so touching. Well, for Mum, it meant everything to her that her elder brothers had loved her small gifts.

To a degree I have kept up the tradition of taking gifts to my dear family members in India since Mum's death, even though they can get everything in India, often of better quality and at lower cost. The gifts have changed and have become much smaller; however, there is one thing that has not changed over the decades: Cadbury dairy milk chocolates.

Even our friends in the US love the Cadbury chocolates. Hubby and I have the same conversation every year as to why I want to give them chocolates when they get them there "Why are you taking them to India and the US?" Every time, the recipients love them because the Cadbury chocolates are not of the same quality in their countries. To this day, I have not had a single person say to me that they don't want them anymore and I know that they're not just being polite to me by accepting them.

All the Successes

Coming back to the opening title of this chapter, my dear reader, that "It is **your** life to celebrate every day (no matter how hard it may be)", I hope that I have given you a glimpse of how true that is. A realisation of the fact that we're on this earth in this incarnation just once – no reruns of it – so we may as well make the best of it, any way we can.

Life is a success if we take it down to the basics and yet these basics make all the difference between having a good life or not. A good life to me is one where I wake up every morning in a warm and comfortable bed, I have a roof over my head, the central heating is on in the winter, the windows are wide open in summer and I am able to jump out of the bed thinking of a good day ahead.

Life is successful when I can eat, drink, talk to people, be with the people I love, do what I want, enjoy being alive and, when things go well, celebrate the wins and successes with a mighty, "YAY!" Have you also noticed how when you have a couple of good things happen in the morning, the rest of the day seems to follow the pattern of things going well? I'm not talking about mega-wins, just things that make one happy. Lots of small wins every day start coming together to become big wins, with life taking on an extraordinarily flourishing look.

Mum survived the atrocities and the pain; she flourished and blossomed into a real matriarch of the family. Her journey was a lot different from mine – and mine is so much different from anyone else's. Our journeys are unique to us. However, the things we all have in common are how we look at life, live and flourish in spite of the setbacks and the dark periods in our lives.

We never thought in our wildest dreams that the three of us would end up in the UK, and that we would not only survive but flourish in our own way. Looking back, numerous stories from the dark times stand out, but to my delight, there are many more of the happier times. The more we learned to be happy and celebrate life's little wins, the more they have kept coming our way.

One of the things my sister and I decided to do was to celebrate Mum's milestone birthdays. These were surprise lunches to which we invited all our friends and family members for Mum's 60th,

65th and 70th birthdays. It was not that much of a tradition to celebrate birthdays for Indian mums at those ages, in such numbers, with a full Gujarati meal, more like a banquet. These were held in community halls so they could hold up to a hundred people at a time. Each time we managed to surprise Mum on some pretext of going to a friend's 'do', and each time she was so happy to see all her family, friends and community people attending the functions. The very last one was the best one ever, even though she was having problems with her diet because, unknown to us, the cancer had already started spreading in April 2002. We had the community friends and elders there, family from afar and neighbours too. One of the neighbours had made a beautiful cake for Mum, there were speeches from the community elders, family and friends, and Mum was presented with a beautiful floral arrangement by the Brahmin Association of Luton. It was truly a memorable occasion.

These wins are having people in our lives, from work colleagues to community friends to family, unexpected connections keep coming to us, adding joy and everyday wins. Friends I would never ever have dreamed of, being from Spain, Poland, Romania, the US, New Zealand, Australia, India and the UK: they just keep coming into my world. I see our friends as an extension of our family. Oh, I nearly forgot to mention the four-legged friends. They keep coming to us, seeking us, no matter where we are, even when we're on holiday in another country.

On a personal and career front, successes have come in the form of good, long careers and writing this book. Did I ever think that I would be writing a book? Not in a million years.

The here and now matters to me; it matters to all of us. However, the journey is equally important to me, if not more. Our life journeys are the making of us, our characters, outlook on life, acceptance of who we are and ambitions. We all dream dreams and that is all part of a good life. We all want to thrive. Nothing has been that easy for us in life until recently and so the journey has left its marks, good and bad. In the main, it has taught us to trust the process, to have faith, be patient and celebrate life any time and every time we can in any way we can. I am a living proof.

One of the successes that has happened recently (January 2021) is that I was selected by the *f:*entrepreneur campaign as one of the top 100 women in small businesses as an inspirational entrepreneur. The hashtag used to identify this special community of entrepreneurs is #ialso100. The Luton and Bedfordshire Chamber was one of the first to promote the story through all its social media platforms and I couldn't have wished for more as it has snowballed from there. I am still being promoted by various media outlets, for which I'm incredibly grateful.

Chapter 3

You Can Still Keep Your Values

You Do Not Have to Lose the Generosity of Your Spirit

Values are what make us as a collective human race, whether as a community bound by religion or ethnicity, in business or as individuals. Our values are from our family, our background and our beliefs, and are ultimately formed by us. I come across a lot through my work about an organisation's values.

As an HR consultant, I often have these conversations with my clients when they are defining their mission or vision statements. The stumbling block is often about what the client as an organisation believes in. How do they even come to define their values? My starting point is, do you know who you are as an individual or as an organisation?

What do you stand for? What standards, values and principles are integrated in the organisation's everyday life, the activities carried out, the interactions with your client and suppliers, and among the employees? Are they congruent to what the organisation stands for, believes in, stands by and is proud to be known for? The values are there every step of the way because in everything we do, they are part of our psyche and behaviour.

When having a difficult time, people often feel that they have to drop their values. That to me is the worst thing anyone can do. I feel that our true personality emerges when we are in a dire situation and we stand by our values; no compromising. In the current economic climate, there is hardship around us; however, have you noticed how people have come together to form all sorts of charities and initiatives to help others less fortunate than they? There are so many different causes that I see on the news and on social media for which people – even children – are raising funds. That is the true generosity of spirit. The values are up there, untarnished.

For me, generosity of spirit means you have a generous heart. It doesn't mean one has to get the wallet out every time. It's just the way one reacts to any situation. My mum was always the first one to be there in any way she could for others. I know a lot of 'careful' people who are lovely, but when it comes to anything charitable, they are not normally the first people to raise their arm. They seem to live in a permanent mindset of scarcity and fear. I really don't understand that mindset of fearfulness.

I haven't had much in life compared to others, and don't have it now, yet I have infinite wealth in my spirit. I'm not a pushover, but I want to give everyone a fair chance without feeling mean about it. The more we give, the more we receive; this is a very simple formula that works beautifully in every sense.

One of the best personal experiences I can think of here is how the people of Luton, our neighbours, who knew nothing about us, took us into their hearts and their world. I think of the little old lady next door, Edna, who used to talk to Mum for hours over the garden fence, exchanging all the news and gardening tips, and their love of flowers. They both loved roses. She would call me over to pick apples from her garden as she was tiny and couldn't reach very high to pick the fruit. The fruit was evenly shared between our family and hers. We were accepted for who we were, the first Asian family in the street, back in 1975. We soon all became very good neighbours and friends.

Then there was another gentleman further up the road who came down to us and did all the painting and maintenance jobs for us, always ready to give us advice or lend a hand with anything that needed going up ladders.

I also think of one of my sisters-in-law in India as an epitome of generosity. She makes time for everyone and has a smile for everyone. Most importantly, she changes so many lives every day, not only because of the work she does as a chief executive of a national charity, but because to her that is true living, true giving and a true purpose of life.

Brahmins are meant to be generous spirited, and I would say that it runs in our family. Mum was always generous spirited. All my aunts and uncles, cousins, very much so. I have been told that I too am generous in spirit.

The Asian community as a whole is generous in spirit; the tiffin or *dabba* movement is well and truly alive wherever they go. A tiffin is a food container, segmented into three or four compartments that fit on top of each other, held together with a long handle. *Dabba* means a box. We like to share our food with family and friends, neighbours and anyone who shows interest in our food; we want to feed them. So basically, the tiffin service involves sharing one's favourite food with others by getting the kids or youngsters to deliver it to family and friends.

In India, especially in Mumbai, the tiffin service is well known for its intricate system of delivering fresh food that is picked up from a person's home and delivered to their workplace anywhere in the city, in time for lunch.

I have been adopted by a lot of the community 'uncles and aunties', especially since Mum died, and so there is a non-stop trail of food parcels. I get a call or message saying, "Bina, I have this tasty dish for you; can you come over and pick it up?" or, "Where have you been? Why haven't you called me? I've been waiting for you. I made something tasty yesterday and thought of you. When are you coming to pick it up?" It's all done with so much love that there is no way to say anything other than, "I'm on my way." I love them all for who they are and how they have filled a big hole in my life.

The easiest option is to have lots of empty ice cream tubs or dabbas that can be washed and reused time and again and given out without worrying about them being returned or the Tupperware boxes that every household has, with at least one large shelf or cabinet in the kitchen full of these recyclable boxes.

Only today I received a lovely Tupperware box full of crab apple chutney, more like a well-known Indian *murabba* – a sweet pickle made of a fruit called *amla* (Indian gooseberry) or mango in syrup with cinnamon, cloves, saffron and other sweet spices. This was a result of a conversation on Facebook with a friend in London asking about ideas to use up a bumper crop of crab apples from a tree in her garden. Before I knew it, some three weeks later, a parcel arrived in the post with this pickle chutney in it.

An elite tiffin service! My entire input to the conversation had been that she could make a *murabba* like my aunt in Mumbai made with these amla, similar to crab apples, which I used to love; and before I knew it she'd said, "Oh, I make a chutney very similar to what you have described and I'll send you some when it's ready!"

Mind you, we all have this inbuilt need in our genes to feed others. There is no escape. A networking colleague was expecting her first baby last year and we got talking about what she liked; before we both realised it, we'd started a home delivery service of cakes, banana and walnut loaves, coffee and walnut loaves, Indian food and pasta made with my special recipes. Food is a universal language that needs no translation when given and received with love: don't you agree?

I love giving surprises when it makes someone's day, such as on the 50th birthday of a friend's wife. Although I hadn't yet met the wife, I felt that I knew her well and wanted to make it a memorable milestone birthday. I ordered a beautiful gift from a well-known quality store in London and with some planning and help from my friend, had it delivered to her for her birthday. She couldn't believe how beautiful the gift was and how I had made her feel on the birthday that she wasn't planning to celebrate. I had a lovely message from her to say that she had a great day, thanks to her family and friends. There you go – a celebration and a day to remember for ever.

Integrity and Honesty

Integrity, honesty, morality, standards and principles are all part and parcel of our being authentic. Who am I? What makes me tick? More importantly, how do I see myself? How do I present myself to others? Am I open, true to myself, without any airs and graces, not compromising on what I stand for?

I was paid a lovely compliment by a sister-in-law when she found out that I was writing a book: she said that it would be human and honest. I hope I live up to it. Integrity is something one doesn't have to worry about because you do not have to hide it.

Integrity and honesty are two aspects of a human being that cannot be hidden. People can tell quickly from your behaviour and the way you treat people whether you have these qualities, whether they can trust you. As you know, it takes time to build trust – but no time at all to lose it.

It also takes time to mend friendships when the trust has been lost, if you're lucky. An incident happened in my hubby's life when he was being made redundant from a position he had in the company, where a close friend of ours worked too. He expected to be backed and supported while he was redeployed to another part of the company. However, he was left to his own devices, even ostracised, and for whatever reason, the support he'd expected was not offered.

The friend realised what she had done a long time afterwards; she had let him down very badly when he had really needed her in his corner.

The trust was broken. It took almost a decade for that friendship to get back to almost its original state. Often, one is not lucky enough to get a second chance in life. Integrity and honesty are such frail creatures; they need looking after very gently.

In life, we are presented with opportunities and challenges every day, at every turn, trying us out as to whether we'll take the easy way out or stick to what we believe in, our morals, our standards and our principles.

In business, I often shy away from people I feel I cannot trust or who seem to have no integrity, even if they could be good clients in terms of income.

I think that most people behave with the best intentions and don't take the easy way out. Sometimes, however, it's the fear of being ostracised or rejected, or of personal loss of some kind, that makes people do the wrong thing. They know that they have taken the wrong decision. Sometimes they don't care. Most of the time, in my experience, people know and do care, but feel they had no option.

I have learned a lot of hard lessons and for me 'easy way out' has never been the answer or the choice. I tend to do it the hard way, which I hope people would say is the right way. Over the past few years, I have also learned that once I have decided that it is a challenge that I have to see it through, somehow it often hasn't been that difficult in the end. As I know only too well by now, I have to trust the process and it will all work out in the end.

Inner Strength and Determination

We all have inner strength, waiting to be discovered, and that little voice of determination saying, "I'm going to try this one more time and win."

The quality of strength lined with tenderness
is an unbeatable combination.

– Maya Angelou

Strength and determination are characteristics that people easily identify in men. When it comes to women, these characteristics or qualities are often berated as negative aspects or undesirable. My maternal grandmother was a force to be reckoned with when it came to strength and determination. My grandfather died at an early age, leaving behind ten children, the youngest just born.

For a widow in the late 1930s in a small village in India, it was a hard life, but my grandmother carried on managing and protecting her family, with her head held high. She was an extremely straight-talking lady, a matriarch with a big heart, full of tenderness. We all loved her for it. I think most of us can identify with this statement in relation to our grandparents or elders in our family.

Her trait of determination and inner strength has passed down the generations. It's evident in the male side of the family, without a doubt, and it is so heartening to see that all the way to fourth generations in the females of the family. Every single one has achieved success in her own right, being role models, breaking new grounds. Just today we learned that one of my nieces, a PhD pharmaceuticals student, has invented a groundbreaking, nanotechnology-based cure for stage 3 lung cancer in India.

Determination is often seen as stubbornness or being obstinate, as a negative trait. To most of us, we need that determination to reach our goals, not to give up at the first hurdle or obstacle. The strength of our willpower comes into play. In our family, we are determined, but often described as stubborn when we think we are right.

I remember an incident when I could have been no more than five or six. Mum, my father and I were visiting my uncle and his family on a Sunday, which we did almost every weekend. We'd spend the day with them and then walk home, which probably took about 45 minutes to an hour. While playing with my cousin outside in their compound, in a wash area with a water tap, where the clothes and utensils were cleaned, I somehow slipped and got totally soaked. My dress and undies were all soiled beyond belief. These had to come off. Mum had not brought any extra clothing with her as it was only a short visit of a few hours.

Well, as you can guess, my aunt offered me my cousin's clothes to put on so I that I could go home in a dry dress. I didn't want any of it; they weren't mine and so it went on and on and on, everyone trying to get me to take the wet clothes off. Even when my father became angry with me, I did not give in. I walked home in it all, a 45-minute walk. I was given a proper Indian bucket bath* when we got home and put on dry clothing. (*An Indian bucket bath involved filling up a large metal bucket with water and using a metal or plastic tumbler with one hand, pouring the water on you, while you soaped yourself and then washing it away with more water. The bucket was kept filled with running water until you had finished.)

I remember that when my sister was young, she could get her own way, most of the time, even with our father. When she was a few years old, she was a very fussy eater, totally opposite to me – I ate anything that was put in front of me. She didn't like the daal with all the spices and coriander leaves floating in it, so would ask Mum to strain it for her. This was totally unheard of and our father used to get very angry with her but she wouldn't budge, even when she was told she wouldn't have any of her meal. In the end, she got her way. All daals were strained for her so the tempering, curry leaves and coriander leaves did not float on the top and she didn't have to eat them. I had seen her take out mustard seeds, cumin seeds and fenugreek of the tempering from vegetables, a bit at a time, using her little fingers, and pile them on one side of her plate.

That stubbornness has stayed with both of us all our lives. I see it in our lives as determination that has got us results, I call it tenacity and perseverance. Mum called it a family trait from my father's side of the family. Hubby says I'm stubborn. Ah well, I know what I call it. The thing is I know I'm always right in most things and that's just how it is. I always joke about it with friends when they'll say in conversation, "Bina, you're right," and I say, "Yes, of course I am," and then we all laugh. It's kind of a joke now.

Joking apart, determination and strength were also aspects of my mum's character that everyone who knew her recognised in her. I've talked about her resilience and determination to carry on through the darkest days of her life.

In the later stages of her life, we knew that Mum was not well. Mum, my sister and I went to see the consultant at the regional hospital for the result of the diagnostic tests. The consultant was looking at me and my sister, saying he had the news. Mum said to him, "Tell me about it, not them. You're telling me about my health."

The consultant thought that Mum was an Indian lady who probably didn't speak English, so he was a bit taken aback. He told her that it was liver cancer and terminal. He asked Mum if she understood what he'd said. She said calmly that yes, she did. She asked how long she had, and was told at the most 12 months. She thanked him and that was it. The consultant then started telling us about all the support that she would be getting from the NHS, Macmillan nurses and so on. We were numb, kind of in a daze.

We came home and it was around 1.30pm. We hadn't eaten so had some tea and toast and some Indian food. My sister and I asked Mum what she would like to do. It was kind of a mechanical, robotic, unreal conversation; I felt as though I would wake up from it all in a minute. Mum was calm and matter-of-fact, as though nothing had happened. "What do you mean? Nothing needs doing. Just carry on."

We asked if she wanted to tell the family, or go to India while she could meet the family, or call them now if she wanted. She told us in a matter-of-fact tone that she didn't want to do any of it. Just carry on living her life as it was. Just normal everyday, simple stuff. No one was going to be told. What could they do as they were thousands of miles away from her? It would only add to their pain and worry. She didn't want that for any of her family. That was the end of the conversation. She did not cry or say, "Why me?" Nothing.

Mum was an incredibly determined woman whose willpower was unwavering. Once she made up her mind about something, no matter how difficult it was, she saw it through. She never gave up. I remember so many instances, but one of the most powerful and lasting events for me was when she was in her last stages of cancer. She had always maintained that the day she could not walk to the bathroom to go to the loo would be the day she would call it a day.

The day came. My sister and I didn't think anything of it when she had to use the bedpan; the social services care assistant was there to manage it all in the bedroom at home. That evening, the care assistant came and helped Mum. I still can see the pain, the humiliation in Mum's eyes as she looked at me while she was helped by the care assistant. For a lady with dignity, pride and morals, that was so very painful and humiliating. Mum did not pass anything after that.

That was a Friday evening. It all suddenly started happening on Friday evening, through to Saturday morning. On Saturday morning, Mum asked me to light the diva, the ghee light for the prayers, and do the *aarti*, even though I was still in my pyjamas and hadn't had my bath. Mum said very clearly to me, "Don't worry, because you are clean in your heart; it's fine, do the *aarti*." I did so; she had a small piece from the *prasad* (an offering from the prayers) of Indian sweets I had bought the previous day. From there on she refused to eat or drink anything. Both my sister and I kept suggesting different food to tempt her to eat but she wouldn't, saying she would a bit later and never did. We both looked at each other, knowing what this meant.

By Saturday evening, Mum's body started having convulsions. The doctor had to give her morphine, on the day of Diwali. On Sunday, New Year's Day, we were getting call after call wishing us *Saal Mubarak*, happy new year greetings from family and friends. We had to disconnect the phone and tell everyone each time that Mum was in the bathroom and she would call back later. I subsequently learned that a lot of the family members suspected that something was not quite right as it was not like Mum at all. Mum died in the early hours of Monday.

Both my sister and I have Mum's legacy of determination. We don't give up. I have been told several times that I am so like Mum, that I sound like her on the phone too.

We have come through a lot and yet, despite the setbacks, we have always looked forward to life being a better life ahead.

Spirituality, Beliefs and Religion

Often our values are determined by the religious beliefs we hold. Faith, God, religion and spirituality are part of our upbringing or we discover them along the way. Often the discovery is the real us. I've been brought up in the Hindu religion and mostly as an outsider looking in. I'm not a traditionalist in the truest sense and so what I believe in, what I know of the religion is all from my own learnings, (just a drop in the ocean), the teachings of the saints, the family and community elders in a mixture of East African, British and Indian Hinduism.

In East Africa, in Uganda, it was how we knew it and perhaps not necessarily totally in synchronisation with the way religion was practised in India. That's not to say that the priests or the good people of the community, the leaders and the pious population didn't do their bit to keep in line with the current scriptures, the rituals, the services, ceremonies and the traditions. Given that we were not in India, it had the East African flair to it. As I mentioned earlier, the Indians had come to East Africa in the earlier part of the 20th century; they had taken their piece of India with them and preserved it through decades while India had moved on in time and was more in step with the modern world in many respects.

It was a similar scenario here in the UK when we arrived in the 1970s. There weren't that many Indian restaurants or temples or shops for that matter, so the pioneering restaurant, Veeraswamy in London, established in 1926 and the Hare Krishna Temple in Watford, established in 1973, were landmarks that Hindus gravitated to on their arrival to the UK if they lived anywhere in the south. My experience of both in the 1970s was the same. We were taken on a grand tour by cousins who had already been living in this country for some time and had been here previously in the 1960s. The awe of finding authentic Indian food in the UK or going to a temple for darshan (a blessing) was exhilarating and memorable.

Over the last 50 years or so, the arrival of East African Asians and the influx of Indians from India in the latter half of the 20th century has changed the dynamics of the Asian population here, which includes communities from Pakistan, Bangladesh and Sri Lanka. The advances in communication and social media have of course played a great part in it. Oddly enough, the distinct communities have come together in many aspects and yet they are disparate too in language, cuisine, mannerisms and traditions.

Sometimes, in general conversation, friends are surprised that I can tell someone's ethnicity from just looking at them, especially Asians. The surnames are also a giveaway as to their origins. With Indians, it is easy to determine even which part of India, which region or state they are from by looking at them or their surname. I often joke with the friends that I know, we all look the same to you.

The Luton Temple started its life in a Gujarati dentist's surgery, in a spare room with a couple of photographs of the deities and half a dozen people having the vision and utter devotion to their religion and Gods to establish a place of worship. I remember many a time we visited the surgery in the evenings for a prayer service. The rest, as they say, is history. The Indian community came together and built the temple. The *mandir* (temple) is not just a place of worship: it represents the community's heart. It's the hub that all roads lead to and from. It's like a church or a mosque, a gurdwara or a synagogue: much more than just a place of worship.

This story has been repeated hundreds of times all over the UK by the Hindu communities. It's the same in any immigrant community that has made its home here. I call this the rich tapestry of life in the UK. Weirdly, when I visit India, I do miss it. I love visiting a few of the temples that are my favourites in India, but the Luton Mandir is home. I feel I belong there, at peace, when I walk in. A sudden calmness comes over me, whether you call it spirituality or just being me. I feel in tune, in harmony with the environment.

The very last night when Mum was conscious, she was kind of going in and out of full consciousness, but she was there enough to answer my questions as to which mandir she wanted us to go to say the final prayers. I asked her if it was the maternal Hanuman Mandir or the Ganesh *mandirs* or some of the ones she loved and had visited in India, and she said in a very clear tone, "None of them, in my Luton Mandir." That was that. So that's what we did; we conducted a virtual prayer service to all the gods in the Luton Mandir, praying to each of them in turn. We carried on through the night and into the morning.

My faith in what I believe has stood me in good stead through good and bad times. It also has been the core of my life, my identity. As I said at the beginning of this subject heading, some of us discover religion, God and our faith along the way. I can vouch for that. Looking back at my life, I was never out of it, but I wasn't deeply informed or aware of it either. It was just there, part of the family, part of our lives. Somehow, over the years, probably more so since Mum died, I seem to have taken over the mantle of the head of the family and all that goes with it, including the faith, beliefs and spirituality. It's almost like a turning point and suddenly I've awakened.

The celebrations, the family traditions, the family values, family honour − all these come together for me through living a life of integrity. MY values have become me, and I have become my values. As a human being, I'm guided by these, every moment of my life, to live as a good human being. When life throws a few curve balls, the strength of my beliefs takes me through. Trusting the process and just letting it be, which brings us back full circle to, "The truth is, you can still keep your values." No matter what life throws at you, dear reader, hold on to your beliefs, values, faith and your God; they will see you through. Often, it is a little test of our faith and patience, that's all: who blinks first. That's all it is.

Chapter 4

You Must Take the First Step to Change Your Life

Hope

"May your choices reflect hope, not fears."

– Nelson Mandela

I can think of many a time when I have hesitated and made a decision out of fear. I think we have all done that because we want the easy way out, not wanting to change the status quo or confront the unknown. I have found that it doesn't really solve much other than postponing the decision. Hope, on the other hand, has given me the feeling of expectation, eternal optimism, of a better life where dreams come true.

Hope as a psychological phenomenon is one way of the heart saying to us that we can get out of the difficult situation by projecting the mind to come up with a better outcome. Hope is the optimism that we feel to get us through a sticky situation.

The point here is that when I haven't seen a way out of a situation or circumstances of ever-downward spiralling thoughts and emotions, I have had to dig deep inside me to find that little voice in my head, and in my heart, that I have the ability, determination, strength, hope, courage, resilience, self-love and intuition to make it happen. The feeling that it is going to be much better there than where I am now. It is hope that keeps me moving forward, a step at a time.

This was most evident when I suddenly had to leave the job that I had loved in my career at the airport; I was good at what I did and suddenly my world came crashing down. It was hope that drove me to dig deep inside me and come up with a solution: to join forces with a business contact in an HR consultancy business. I had never imagined that I would ever be leaving the airport the way I left –

but that's life. It was a tough time and perhaps more stressful in some ways even than leaving Uganda. I am eternally hopeful and to be honest, it has always been hope that has looked after me.

Hope has been an overriding factor in most people's lives; it gives us that warm feeling about good outcomes from our actions, dreams and ambitions. Faith in it happening goes hand in hand with hope. Never has that been truer than in these unusual times of 2020 and 2021, when the world has stood still in so many ways.

We as human beings have had to sit up and take notice of something much more powerful than us, controlling our lives. While we have had to totally change our behaviour and thinking about the earth, our environment, our freedom and everything about how we live our lives, hope and faith are two things that have kept us going, dreaming and expecting to emerge into a better world. A classic example of this, as I write, is the world changing as the US election results were announced on 7 November 2020; people around the world once more saw hope not just for the US but for the whole world.

When I look back at Mum and me, over the years, including when we were in Uganda, I know that hope and faith kept us moving. Hope of knowing, feeling the ambition rising in me that I deserved better than this. I knew I could make it happen and that I would be supported. Hope and faith have always been the supporters of my dreams and my ambitions. Although I never defined what was driving me through tough times, it was that eternal optimism and hope, mixed with my stubbornness, that I would succeed.

In recent years, understanding more about myself and the way things work for me when I focus on the outcomes, and most of all, the faith in knowing that I'm being supported, has seen me through. I accept the fact that sometimes it's not a straight line to achieving a good outcome; more often than not, it's a bit of a zigzag path to my destinations, but hey, I get there. That's all that matters.

Have you noticed how once you decide to take action, no matter how small it is, things fall in place? Have you also noticed that people and events appear to make it happen? The right people in the right place at the right time. Have you also noticed that procrastination or the thought of tackling something difficult or unknown is in effect more stressful than actually doing it? It's not that bad at all once you take a deep breath and go for it.

This has been my experience every time. I think of the times when I wanted to go for a new job or had to say something difficult to someone. It's made me realise that our mind often works as the prohibitor, the mischief-maker in the scenario when the little voice in your heart and soul is just saying that it's OK, keep going. I no longer listen to the mind, just the heart. My intuition, hope and faith are the drivers.

Over the past year, during the pandemic, my business has flourished. By being open to ideas, I was recently selected by the *f:*entrepreneur campaign, which highlighted inspirational business leaders across the UK, as one of the top 100 businesswomen (#ialso100) for 2021. I had never expected to receive so much support, love and admiration from so many people, even from unexpected sources. I have been totally overwhelmed by it all.

Courage

Susan Jeffers' book, *Feel the Fear and Do it Anyway*, was published over 25 years ago, and its message is still as fresh now as it was back then.

Over the years this has also become my motto: I do feel the fear to start with, but then just focus on the outcome and do it anyway. What's the worst that can happen? Funnily enough, I was one of those people who would have a great dialogue in my head about asking someone something, especially in business or at work in my corporate days.

I would have all the nays in my head as to how the other person was going to turn me down. Worse still, I felt the inadequacy of myself, little me; why would they want to say yes to me? You know what, that's all changed in the last few years, in that I now have a simple approach. What's the worst that could happen? They say no? However, there could be a lot more outcomes than a straight no. Even if they did say no, could I handle it? It works every time.

A classic example is a simple thing like putting forward a client proposal in my current business. In the early days, I used to worry about every little thing, about why they would say no to me, and now I don't worry about it at all. I do all the hard work, make sure I have covered everything I need to get the client on board but then, once the proposal's gone, that's it. No worrying about it. It works most times for the best reasons for both parties. The relationship starts off as an equal partnership.

Going back to our days in Uganda, in the days when it was unheard of for Indian women to strike out on their own, away from the family home, there were three of us who made that decision. The future ahead was uncertain, not knowing how, where or when we'd be able to make that move. What was certain in our hearts was that we could not stay where we were in the way we were and so it had to happen. Mum's fortitude kept us going.

The change had to happen. I've touched on this before, that when faced with an existence and all it was full of fear and torment, we had to break away from it for good. We had to break the chain. Mum and I used to often talk about it when we were on our own, and we used to say to each other "that change had to happen for you, me and her".

Asians were expelled from Uganda by the dictator, Idi Amin, in 1972. As you probably remember, Asians had been brought to Uganda in East Africa by the British, when India and East African countries including Kenya and Uganda were British colonies. After Kenya and Uganda gained independence in the 1960s, Uganda was a stable country until Idi Amin toppled the government in a coup in 1970. He decided that he did not want any Asians who hadn't taken Ugandan citizenship and they had to leave. The expulsion order came in August 1972 for Asians holding any other passports, mainly Indian, Pakistani or British.

The Asians and the world politicians thought he couldn't be serious; surely it was a joke. It wasn't. It reminds me of some of the politicians today; there are similarities. It became very apparent soon enough that it was not a joke when the dusk-to-dawn curfew came into force, and the streets were patrolled by soldiers day and night. At night, not only did they loot the households, but also carried out rapes and murders.

None of us slept much during those months. We'd hear the army lorries patrolling the streets, and were petrified of every sound coming from the road outside, praying hard for the lorries not to stop outside our house.

One night, we heard shouting and screaming coming from our neighbour's house but we were helpless to do anything. We found out in the morning that the soldiers had looted the place and when they saw a young girl, they were about to rape her when her young brother threw himself at the soldier, who was carrying a rifle in his hand, begging him to spare her. This was a 7-year-old boy asking for mercy for a 14-year-old sister. For whatever reason, after a minute or two of looking at the boy, the soldier put his hand on the boy's head and walked out of the room.

Then there were the times in the morning, when the Asian men were going to work, the soldiers would stop their jeep by the houses, order the men to get in the jeep and that was the last that anyone would see of the men. The residents in the area that we lived in were mainly upper-middle-class Asians, business owners who then became a perfect target for rich pickings for the soldiers.

When it did happen, the way it happened with Idi Amin, the Asians with British Indian or non-Ugandan passports were given three months or 90 days to leave Uganda, from 4 August to the end of 8 November 1972, if they didn't have Ugandan citizenship. Our family and our extended family on my father's side were going to the UK because they held British passports.

My father wanted to live in India, but we didn't because Mum did not want to burden her brothers or any of the family. We saw this as our chance to break away, so Mum and I made it very clear to my father that we would remain in the UK once we got there, whereas he was going to continue his journey from the UK to India. We were not going to go with him to India. My father was sure that we wouldn't last on our own for long. He was certain that we would be begging him soon afterwards to let us join him in India. I have no idea how he agreed in the first place, but he did. I only thank our stars and destinies that he allowed us to do that.

It was a very strange time in every way. Again, on the surface, it was all fine; underneath, it was a total bedlam of emotions. We were frightened, relieved and hurt that we were being forsaken, that we were not wanted or loved and that we had to make our own way. This was especially an extremely terrifying time for my young sister, who was at an impressionable age, to such an extent that she had nightmares for the first few months after being in the UK.

Nevertheless, we were also determined that we would be happy in our own way and make it a success.

The emotions were all over the place, not only because we were leaving everything behind in Kampala; we left the house open and walked out with a suitcase each and £50 for the four of us. We were also going to be fending for ourselves for the first time very soon. It is definitely a very strange feeling, almost like learning to walk and talk, to think for ourselves for the very first time, not having to worry about the repercussions or needing that permission.

There was also the fact that we had to show courage in the face of dictatorial treatment from the army. We didn't know whether we were going to get on the plane to Heathrow. The coach that we were on, organised by the British Embassy, was stopped a couple of times on the road from Kampala to Entebbe Airport. It was only a 20-mile journey, but seemed like an eternity.

On reaching the airport, we were shepherded to the check-in hall and then sent separately from the men to security, escorted by army soldiers strutting around with their guns. Even when we were searched in security, the soldiers were very much present in the women's area, checking what we were wearing, what jewellery we had on, smirking and just being that little bit menacing.

We weren't sure whether we were ever going to get to the aircraft, all under the escort of the soldiers. I remember so clearly the anxiety and fear on everyone's faces as the plane started taxiing down towards the one runway, wondering whether it was going to be called back to the stand or if it would actually take off. Everyone breathed an audible sigh of relief when at long last we were on board and the plane took off. People were praying, holding it all together. I can only describe it as finding courage and strength from our faith. Hope, faith and fortitude all played their part for sure.

Resilience

> *"I can be changed by what happened to me,*
> *but I refuse to be reduced by it."*
>
> – Maya Angelou

How true! We all have gone through some tough times that shaped us in some way. When anyone finds out a bit more about me or my background, even just about my being a refugee from Uganda, I know that they are amazed by it, especially how I have come to be where I am now. Then again, that is so true about everyone's past. Everyone has a story to tell, which unless you ask them, you would never know.

Resilience for me has been that absolute willpower to override any difficulties and tough circumstances, to spring back and keep smiling.

We lived a double life for many years: one a public one, where everything was OK; and the other one, which was stifling, restrictive, hurtful and often traumatic. My father was an upstanding community family man and had a good job at the Attorney General's office, earning a good salary. The community at large saw him as a man who was good looking and generous, with a sense of humour, and who loved playing badminton. So he had a badminton grass court made in our garden where the neighbourhood men and youngsters played every evening for a couple of hours. We were not part of that scene. We were not allowed to go anywhere near the court or even say hello to them.

In the evening, the three of us used to go for a walk to my paternal aunt's place or quite often go to the library. We lived near the parliament building, so would go for a walk near there in the grounds where there was a large public park and the public library nearby. Although we had English language and literature books at school, this was different. Mum and I discovered all sorts of English books, from *Anne of Green Gables* to the works of Zane Grey and Neville Shute. We also discovered Mills & Boon romances, murder mysteries, the works of Shakespeare and English classics, including those written by P G Wodehouse. My sister, then at a young age, discovered her age books. This was our escape from everyday stuff happening around us, and to us.

A couple of years ago, my hubby and I were in Brooklyn, New York, at Barnes & Noble, the famous book shop. I suddenly saw a beautifully bound copy of *Anne of Green Gables*, engraved and with gold leaf edging on the pages. So many memories of this book came flooding back to me as I picked it up. I was smiling and feeling so emotional about it. Well, I bought it for old times' sake; it's a treasured book. Funny enough, it fits right in here, doesn't it, with Anne's fortitude and unbreakable loving spirit, along with her green hair, which makes me smile every time I think of it and how all three of us have always had a special place in our hearts for this book. I also remember the time when there was a TV series in the mid-1970s, based on the book. It was shown on a Sunday afternoon, and all three of us used to sit there glued to the programme.

I have always loved listening to family elders talking about their past, about when they were young and what they had to go through. All these have a common thread of hard work, bringing up families, carrying out domestic chores from early morning to late at night with not much in the way of luxuries. Yet they all flourished and brought us up to be independent and resilient.

I love connecting with people in life and it has become part of my life as a businesswoman – networking and connecting with other businesses is part of being in business. Often this entails a one-to-one session or having a coffee to get to know someone a bit better, having met them at a networking event, or as it so often happens now, on an online Zoom networking meeting.

The intention is to see if there is synergy between the two businesses, whether we can help each other and most of all, whether we like and identify with each other having similar values and outlook on business and life. This is where the stories come out and I see that resilience of having come through some horrendous times, still standing, smiling and alive to tell the story.

I have worked a lot with women over the years, through my corporate life, current business and in the community. In all these areas, I have known several women for whom I have nothing but admiration, for how they have lived their lives. There are so many stories, so many cases of hardship, and yet so many of these women are smiling through life, still standing as winners after having suffered their life-threatening illnesses, a family member's ill health, or other life tragedies.

Women are finding their voice and strength to stand up for their own rights more and more through the decades and yet there are still so many women who have no life of their own. They are restricted in every possible way, by parents, husbands, brothers, other family members, religion, traditions and doubting their own self-worth. This is where I want to reach out and say to them that if we could do it without any resources, you can certainly do it now.

All you need is the resilience and courage to walk away from it, just as we did decades ago, because the current situation is not serving you and your dreams.

Self-Love

Self-love is not a term that many Indian women knew or understood when I was growing up. To think of oneself, to be kind and considerate, and to put oneself before everyone else in the family. In fact, I don't think many women would have known the term until recently. This includes thinking of walking away from anything and everything for their sanity, happiness and the right to live a free life.

Like all little girls, I was taught to think of others first, to share first before thinking of myself. Sharing and giving comes very easily in Indian communities, so when one doesn't, one is labelled as selfish or made to think that one needs to change one's ways. Most girls automatically became a lot like their mums, putting others first.

It was a lot more like that when I was growing up. A lot of this was centred around food, especially like a bar of Cadbury dairy milk chocolate: it was unheard of to eat a bar all by yourself. All the pieces were shared out, with you taking the last one. It was the same with any food; for instance, if there was one last portion left, you didn't help yourself, but offered it round the table to anyone who wanted it.

The women were always the last to eat, often not having enough for themselves. The men came first. The tradition has always been that the men have their meal first, then the kids along with the men or before the men and last, the women. Most families thankfully now eat together, but the hierarchy remains. The men and kids will get served before the women.

Years afterwards, when we were all grown up, Mum would still tell us to take the last portion as she didn't want it. This didn't work with me once I was old enough to say no and put the last portion on her plate. I think all mums are born like that and don't change until the end, always thinking of others first.

So, when it comes to self-love, to put oneself first, it often means almost reprogramming the brain to think differently. At the age of 12, I had to do this for Mum, my sister and me. I realised that we could not go on the way we were. I think I have always been a bit naïve in ways of the world; however, this was one situation where I wasn't slow on the uptake, wanting to be free of a controlling environment. Our decision was very focused on being somewhere, anywhere that gave us a peaceful present and a hopeful future.

Something happened this week that reconfirmed my belief in thinking of myself first. It meant holding on to my integrity and values in the face of challenges and having the guts to say, "Enough is enough." It is about self-preservation and peace of mind too.

I had a client whom I took on a while ago, against my better judgment and gut feeling, but I did anyway. Recently, we had the same conversation over and over for a long period about what they could and couldn't do about employees, taking into account compliance and fairness. Each time it was the same: they would try to get things done in a way that suited them but was not right. There was an incident where it was evident that the decision they wanted to take wasn't fair and correct; once again I advised a course of action and once again, they wanted to do it differently, totally contrary to my advice. I walked away from it all, and terminated my contract with them.

This event has made me think about why, despite knowing that it wasn't good for my peace of mind, I carried on. Even at this ripe old age, the lifelong subconscious training of thinking of others first made me persevere.

On a cheery note, I love to watch my little nieces and nephews growing up with a very balanced view of life. There is that very cheeky and innocent way they get what they want, with an overload of cuteness. It's that clarity and focus on their decision-making that leaves me quietly applauding and cheering them. Some may call it being precocious: I call it self-love, a true positive aspect of their personalities.

Chapter 5

It's Easier to Make That Change Than to Stay as You Are

Change

Throughout my work life over the decades, I have often been told that one thing that is guaranteed in life is change. Change always happens. Expect change to happen so embrace it in a big hug; don't resist it. In the world of business, and work, many people have made successful careers out of 'change management', systemising change, making it a way to move forward. Our lives evolve constantly through change, sometimes with our blessing and sometimes with our reluctance, but it happens. Life has taught me to just hold on, see it through, trust the process. It'll be better for me in the end.

There are many of us who want to stay as we are, in our safe environments. Most times though, when we look back at the change that has happened to us, we see that it has been positive. I know of so many people who were made redundant from their corporate roles, jobs they really didn't like but stayed in for the fear of the unknown, for the security of a regular income.

When they were made redundant, it was tough to begin with, as it always is. Once they got to grips with it though and accepted the fait accompli, they started their businesses based on something they were passionate about, perhaps a hobby or something for which they had seen a gap in the market. I've often mentored men and women during this change and seen them come through the other side.

When I was at the airport as head of HR, there were always changes: in management or the infrastructure, the modernisation of the airport, the new technology and innovations in aviation. All of these brought change to the way the airport operated. That of course meant change to people's lives and livelihoods. On one occasion, a huge restructuring change affected hundreds of people across the airport.

They were tough times for everyone who wanted the change and for those who didn't, working side by side, and then some wanting to leave because they did not like the new way of working. Some of those who left found a new lease of life doing their own thing, opening businesses that they had wanted to try out, such as working as a carpenter or decorator, setting up a family outdoors mini-adventure park, travelling the world or retiring in the sunny climes of Spain.

Looking back at my life, I don't think I ever stood still and thought of it as "Ooh, that's another change come my way." It's just a journey; life is where things happen, sometime good, sometimes it could be better but hey, it's life. As I have got older, I have learned to go with the flow. That expression has become a mantra for me; don't resist the change. This doesn't mean that I haven't resisted change in my life, fought it, and tried my best to maintain the status quo, but every time it has been futile. Now, having learned the lessons, I welcome change.

Change has brought joy, excitement, new opportunities and, most of all, new people in my life who wouldn't have been there were it not for the change in my circumstances. Talking of people, such lifelong friendships have developed for me throughout. People come and go in our lives; some stay the duration of the course, such as my friend from my college days, when I was 17, who is still in my life.

We have come through the different stages of life, from being at college and in a girls' hostel in Mumbai to emigrating to the UK, raising families and seeing kids who in turn have their offspring. She came from Kenya: I from Uganda. We met each other's families for the first time in the UK in 1973 and took to each other straight away.

Thus, the friendship blossomed between the two families, I have seen my friend's young siblings from being of school age to becoming grandparents. The constant is our friendship. Although we don't speak to each other every day or see each other as often as we'd like, the friendship has remained strong.

The people from different countries who are in our lives as friends are all there because of change – in their circumstances or my hubby's and mine. I love the way people arrive in my world, our world, often with not much in common at all and yet, over time, that all changes and we become friends, in the US, Poland, Spain, the UK or India.

I call them our global families because that's what they are: an extension of our family from different parts of the world. Never in my wildest dreams would I have thought that I would have friends from different countries around the world. I have a large extended family in India, as I have mentioned before, and with the rise of social media have made many more friends over the last eight or nine years, some of them very close friends.

There is the young lady from Mumbai with whom I started exchanging tweets a few years ago. In the beginning, I realised that she was stamping her personality all over Twitter through her tweets. Anyway, we started chatting and then we were having normal conversations and became friends. We tried to meet every trip I was in Mumbai and for some reason it wasn't until 2017 that I met my friend in person for a few minutes. My cousin sister and I met her for a little while. We kept chatting, and a couple of years ago, she married a lovely young man.

In early January 2019, on another of my trips to India, we arranged to meet in Mumbai. Having travelled around, as I tend to do on these trips, visiting my family members who are scattered around mainly in Gujarat, Maharashtra and Bangalore, I returned to Mumbai. For some reason, it was just not possible for us to meet in the end as she had to travel out to another part of India.

She arranged to have a gift she had bought for me to be delivered to my cousin's place at the other end of the city. With the Indian tenacity of getting things done, once they make up their mind, it was ready and waiting for me when I arrived at my cousin's home through a number of arrangements made between my friend, my cousin brother and me.

Thinking it would be a small gift, I soon realised from the size of the package that it definitely was not. I unwrapped the parcel, all beautifully wrapped in orange patterned wrapping paper, and opened the box to reveal the most exquisite orange silk sari, with fuchsia pink border, all hand embroidered in gold and silver. I was stunned, totally humbled to have been gifted such an expensive sari.

When I messaged her soon after, all babbling now with excitement and happiness, she told me that she wanted me to have something special in my favourite colour, orange. The sari was so beautiful that she had ordered one for herself too and said that we would have to wear ours together at our next meeting as terrible twins. My generous friend is less than half my age, more like a niece. I wore the sari in 2020 at a nephew's wedding in India and alas once again, I could not meet my dear friend in Mumbai as she was travelling elsewhere in India while I was there.

One of the Polish friends working with Ian at the airport just became part of the family over the years, to the point that her daughter calls me *Ciocia* or Auntie. Once again, the little girl is the apple of our eyes; I have seen her grow up since she was a baby. The whole family is now our family, to the extent that we are in contact every day, just as families do.

Another friend who stayed with us for a while, due to change in her personal circumstances, came into our lives and luckily stayed. Once again, happily, she has become very much part of the family.

I often say jokingly that we welcome all waifs and strays into our home and into our lives: two-legged, four-legged – all are welcome!

Many of our US friends became so through Ian's love of cycling and visiting Pennsylvania over a number of years for the epic cyclo-cross race he so enjoys riding. We were welcomed from day one, even though they didn't know us at all, and very quickly became close friends. The couple we stayed with at their bed and breakfast inn in deepest rural Pennsylvania were so generous in every way. Alas, both the husband and wife died recently; we miss them so much. They were not just the perfect hosts, but their generosity knew no limits. They loved people, and anyone fortunate to meet them, loved them.

Loved them both to bits. What a beautiful place they had – and their cats! As cat lovers, we loved their kitten the first year we were there. The kitten had no name. I loved the name Rosie, which I suggested to the lady of the house. So Rosie she became, this little kitten who grew into a huge furry ball of a cat and whom we saw every October for several years.

They were such fun times, exchanging stories about the British and American cultures and their respective idiosyncrasies, which were loveable, yet at times unfathomable. Why is a light switch upside down in America? When you want to switch on the light, you push the switch up instead of down.

The lady of the house, Mary Ellen, was a brilliant cook and she used to make all the vegetarian options for me. Her baking was amazing. Breakfasts were a grand affair with all the trimmings, and every day there was a different freshly baked cake or some fruit muffins and biscuits (what we would call plain scones in Britain). Over the years, Mary Ellen and Allan became such good friends that we had the run of the house, just like visiting our family.

Social media brought and keep bringing so many wonderful people into my life. During the early years of the business in a partnership, a business coach made it clear that we had to embrace social media, get on to Twitter and LinkedIn. This was another change that I embraced very quickly, especially Twitter. It has connected me to a global community of HR professionals and lots of great connections, business and personal, one of them being the lovely young lady who gifted me the silk sari. Embracing change is a choice, of course.

Choices

We all have choices even though we don't think we do. The clarity of our thoughts gives us control over the choices we make, the decisions we take. It's always either/or, which makes all the difference in it being the right or the wrong choice. Gut feeling comes into it just as much as looking at the facts that we have. It is still that weighing up of probabilities of one or the other, or perhaps a number of options open to us, that gets us to our chosen path.

In the earlier chapter, I touched on the fact that one has to take that first step to change one's life. "I choose to be happy," has become one of the all-time favourite mantras in our modern lives. It may seem a bit odd to many readers and yet, the words hold that wholesomeness in them that "I choose to be happy… (no matter what) and of my free will. I choose to be happy because I can deal with anything life throws at me because I'm choosing to be happy."

Well, I have chosen to be happy. It means that whatever action I have to take to stay happy, be happy, then that is in my hands to do so. It also means that when any situation no longer serves me, I have to find a way to get out of it, change it or deal with it, as I'm the one to make it happen.

A lot of people have commented about my smile. I learned a long time ago that no matter what's happening in my life, the world doesn't want to see my glum face, especially at work. That is the work mask that goes on. However, most times it's a smile of feeling happy, feeling great to see someone I know, that feeling of connectivity as you look at someone, they see you, and the acknowledgement of being human, you both smile. Well, I do anyway. It's a reflex action. I like smiling.

The more I have smiled over the years, the more I've had to smile about. Also, smiling is so infectious. I find it very easy to smile. It becomes a bit tricky at times, especially on public transport. I just don't know how people who travel every day on the same train, catching the train at the same time, sitting in the same compartment in their same seats don't even acknowledge or smile at one another. It's just a common courtesy, isn't it?

For all the hellos and good mornings, I love being in Yorkshire. As we head up the M1 or the M6, depending on which route we take, we come off the motorway at the junction of Lancaster. To me, that's the beginning of our adventures in Yorkshire, the beautiful countryside with charm of its own, the rolling hills, the stark mountains, the sheep grazing in the fields, the stone houses and the vast open spaces.

I fell in love with Yorkshire when in the late 1990s hubby started cyclo-cross racing again there in the Yorkshire Dales, especially around the Settle and Ingleton area. Everyone you meet in the

Dales will say, "Hello," or "Ey oop" – well the locals do anyway. I automatically want to say, "Hello" to everyone I meet there; hubby just rolls his eyes at me for doing that.

I have always associated Yorkshire with cold weather, probably because we've always been up there in autumn. However, it makes up for this tenfold by being warm-hearted; the people are very friendly, and I love their gorgeous Yorkshire accent. The food is wholesome, there is a feeling of wholesomeness about the place that I love. It's not quaint but a rugged, beautiful, welcoming friend.

On the other hand, time and again, it has become apparent to me that when that feeling starts coming over me that the situation is not to my liking or it is not helping me, I now don't hesitate to make a decision. I feel very strongly that if a situation needs addressing, then it's up to me. Letting go of anything that doesn't serve me has given me a feeling of freedom. I've learned it the hard way, but better late than never, to be honest. If I can do it, you can, anyone can.

Having seen what Mum went through, I now don't see life as a sentence. Life is to be enjoyed, to be cherished and celebrated at every opportunity. The choice is mine, yours, ours. How we choose to be. I have found that agonising over a decision is much tougher than just going for it. Whatever decision I make, it turns out OK and most times more than OK.

I mentioned before that inner dialogue is such a mischief-maker, a prohibitor, giving all the excuses as to why I shouldn't, a saboteur. In the past, it used to be a decision taken in fear; what-ifs played a big part. Now, I just go for it. It works very well every time. It's so much better than staying as I am in that agonising phase of life, arguing with myself.

One of the major choices we made in our lives was to come to the UK instead of going to India. I'm sure we'd have managed there too, as I can say now that we are survivors. I'm not sure what kind of life it would have been. All the same, I wouldn't have been sitting here typing away our story or met my hubby or all the lovely people I have along the way. The decision was the right one for us. Our destiny was here in the UK.

All the career paths I've chosen have come from choices which seemed right at the time and, to be honest, have served me well. Every single one arose when one door was closing; as I have said before, another one was already open. Someone in my life was there for me, instrumental in making it happen for me.

Take the time when I was working for the package tour and airline company Court Line Aviation, in my first job in the UK. Suddenly we were told that they were going to bring in a computer system, so being a junior data processing clerk, I might not have a job. I'd been there for only about 18 months. A young lady in my department had joined us about six months after I'd started. Linda was from New Zealand on a working holiday-cum-pilgrimage to Blighty – as many young New Zealanders wanted to do – basically backpacking, working and seeing their old forefathers' country.

She and her friend had run out of money while they were in Crawley, so stuck a pin on a map with a 50-mile radius, I think. It landed on Luton. They arrived in Luton by coach from Gatwick Airport and soon found jobs in a pub near the airport. Linda saw a job advertised in the local paper and hey presto, she joined us. Another bubbly individual; all three of us became friends and still are, to this day.

Going back to the story about jobs and people, Linda wasn't bothered too much about losing her job if a new computer came in as she was returning home with a British hubby. She saw in the local paper that the Luton Telephone Exchange was advertising for telephone operators at the local exchange and suggested that I apply for one of the jobs, telling me how wonderful a telephonist's job was in New Zealand – with all the glamour of working with the Flying Doctors.

All this Mills & Boon story stuff about Flying Doctors was enough for me to apply and there I was, in a huge telephone exchange in the main telephone switchboard hall with about 70 other female switchboard operators or telephonists using the old plugging in connection system. I should say here that I'd been in the job for only a couple of months at the telephone exchange when we heard that the airline company Court Line Aviation had gone into liquidation overnight. It shocked all of us in the town as it was a major company at the airport. The divine intervention by my Kiwi friend Linda took me to another successful career path with British Telecom, which was part of the Post Office until it became a separate public corporation in 1981.

Trust Yourself

It has been a long while, going forward, trusting myself to make the right decisions, standing up for myself and knowing that it's always going to be OK. To begin with, trusting myself to make the change came as a shock to the system. Every time my career changed, there was a decision involved on the basis that a door was shutting on me. I have been very lucky or perhaps unconsciously I made the right decisions.

I remember the first time I went for an interview at the airport. I had been in the UK for four weeks in a totally new environment: cold, an alien town where every street looked the same, uniform brown-bricked terraced houses with only the different coloured doors providing any individuality. A cousin drove me in his car to the interview. I met a very pleasant, affable gentlemen in his early 50s, over six-foot tall, looming over me. He asked me a few questions and inquired whether I could start the following week. That was that.

The job was that of a junior data processing clerk in an airline company, at a grand salary of something like £54 a month. This was a great pay rise after the first four weeks when I had to queue up for a handout of £5 a week at the local unemployment benefit office, known as the dole office – a totally humiliating experience of having to sign on a dotted line to be given money. I still remember the Portakabin – cold, musty, with a smoky atmosphere.

The friendly lady at the counter smiled, explained everything and spoke slowly so that I could understand what she was saying. She checked that I had understood. My written English was fine, and since I had been taught by a number of British and American teachers in Kampala, I could understand clear, precise textbook English; however, listening to fast speech in Lutonian accents around me was another thing altogether. She had obviously had plenty of practice speaking to non-English claimants. I was grateful that she understood our plight.

The airport job was an exciting adventure. I borrowed a dress from my niece, who was of the same build as me, as I didn't have any dresses. I used to wear the salwar kameez, Indian suits of cotton leggings and tunic tops. That's another story for another chapter. I was very skinny at the time, a mere size 10.

In the 1970s, minis and platform shoes were the height of fashion. It wasn't the done thing to wear the Indian trouser suit at work at the time, especially in an office environment. During that first month, I borrowed a couple of dresses that my cousin and niece could spare, wearing them alternately until Mum, my sister and I could go to town to buy some clothes after my first pay day. I still remember my first heavy woollen coat in a burgundy colour. It was a far cry from and so much warmer than the heaviest woollen cardigan I had brought over from Uganda, one that was of such loose knit that it was totally useless in the cold autumnal weather.

Trusting myself – ourselves as it were for the three of us – was an exercise in itself. I have realised over time that it comes from within: the prompting, assurance and certainty. When in doubt, looking within has helped. Mum always knew what she wanted and when she'd made up her mind, that was then going to happen, without a doubt.

She had obviously trusted herself enough to want to start a new life in a new country with no financial support from anyone. She could have taken the easy way out by turning up at her brothers' homes with two daughters. She chose the harder path because that was the right thing to do. Her pride and her trust in herself, in her faith, helped her make that decision. This is what it comes down to, looking within, being brutally honest to ourselves in carrying out a true self-assessment and giving ourselves credit that we are a lot stronger than we think we are. We always find that extra bit of strength that takes us to that desired outcome.

Go With the Flow

One of the life lessons I have learned over time is to go with the flow. It wasn't always so. Depending on how difficult the situation was or how much it was hurting me emotionally, as the saying goes, someone occupying my head without paying the rent. That's when something had to be done.

Mum was always very patient, all the way through her life, whereas I was totally the opposite in my younger days. I just wanted it done, there and then, wanted to know the outcome. It didn't matter how trivial it was. It could be something simple, such as waiting for a service provider to call back on a query or a service arrangement; I would be mentally pacing up and down for them to call. Or if I had left a message for a family member to call me back, I wanted to know why they hadn't. I'd be chuntering on about why they hadn't called, and Mum would often say to me, "Just sit quietly, will you?"

To some degree, I'm still like that. Life has taught me one very big lesson though: when I chase people or things, they keep running away from me; when I don't and let it be, go with the flow, it works out. People are chasing me or rather they come to me. I no longer get anxious about any outcomes that I'm waiting for; they all work out in the end.

A funny thing happened yesterday when a very close friend of ours, Berni, asked me about my progress in writing this book. I commented to her that I hadn't been sure about it at all until I had the feedback I'd been waiting for from my coach, which was all fine. I was given my own medicine as Berni quietly sent me the message, "Trust the process!". I'm often the one telling her that. So funny! Just loved it and it brought home that she was totally right to remind me of it. Go with the flow by trusting the process. There you go, all sorted.

The 'go with the flow' philosophy has also taught me to see life more benevolently, with a gentler outlook and disposition towards everyone and everything. It has calmed me down a lot, with the assurance that it's going to all work out, so why worry? Where perhaps I would have been angry, anxious or impatient, I have learned to view it with a quiet expectation and eagerness.

A quaint story comes to mind of Mum's philosophy of taking it easy, going with the flow. There used to be a pick-your-own-fruit farm near St Albans that we visited every year in the summer months when the strawberries were in abundance, along with other soft summer fruits, such as raspberries, gooseberries and currants. Our favourite were the strawberries.

I would have the big basket, the punnet that the farm owner would give us to collect the strawberries, which were sold by the weight. Well, I'd be picking the strawberries, nice ripe ones for us to take home, while Mum would be strolling around, picking the biggest, most luscious strawberries she could find and popping them in her mouth. I'd tell her off not to eat any there and Mum would say, "Don't worry, I'll tell them to charge us for the extra ones I've eaten on top of the ones in the punnet." She did and the farmer never charged us any extra. They knew how these farms worked and I'm sure it was all included in the price for the ones in the punnet.

The whole aspect of knowing that it's easier to make the change than stay as I am has proved time and again that the next stage of my evolution is waiting for me. It's always going to keep happening, with or without me accepting it, embracing it. What have I got to lose? Actually, nothing, and everything to gain. Beata Pawlikowska, a Polish writer, reminded me yesterday, "Why would I want to stay as I am when the world is moving on?"

Just looking at our own lives, we all use new technology as it evolves, even with a simple thing like telephones. How far have we come in using mobile phones? Some ten to 15 years ago, the fixed landline telephone was used more commonly than mobiles in our homes and for business. Now, most of us can't be without our mobiles near us during our waking hours.

We wouldn't want to stay with the old technology, the old ways of communication, transport, food, the way we do business or watch entertainment. Anything and everything keeps changing, giving us better life experiences. The choice is always ours. Going with the flow is so much better and easier than going against it, don't you think?

Chapter 6

You Must Believe in Yourself (Be True to Yourself)

Taking Action

Every step of the way in my life, there have been quite a few scenarios which I would have never dreamed of in a million years. An Indian girl from Kampala with a strict Gujarati upbringing, who did not dare speak to a man or anyone outside our family unless I was given permission to – suddenly in the UK and working a weekly shift system, including night shifts in a mainly male dominated environment in a computer centre. It certainly was an education in itself.

Hard work has never frightened me, Mum or my sister and so it's always been a way of life. Long hours of work or travelling at odd hours of the day and night never bothered me in as much as they were just experiences that I had to get on with, take action and progress. When I was working as a telephonist at the Post Office (which had both the postal and telecommunications sides of the business), many of the towns in the UK were not on automated dialling, and so a telephonist had to connect the calls.

I was one of the telephonists who did that. I also worked on the emergency services as well as directory enquiries; the caller dialled 100 for the operator, 192 for directory enquiries to find a telephone number for a contact anywhere in the UK whose full name and address was required before the number was given out, or 999 for emergency services. You may have seen old films where a telephone operator with a cord in her hand and a headset plugged into the switchboard said, "Number please?" That could have been me. Oddly enough, even now I remember most of the dialling codes of UK main towns and cities.

Well, as the exchanges were automated, the requirement for the operators became less frequent. Modernisation brought new career opportunities. As the Post Office at the time had the postal services and much more across the country, being a large national organisation, one could apply for a transfer to a totally different part of the business or part of the country.

I decided to go for computing. There was a computer centre in another town nearby. I had to sit a battery of tests at the regional office in Essex, all of which I passed. I was offered a junior data processing officer position on shift in the computer centre in St Albans, near Luton. The money was good, but involved working three shift patterns on a weekly basis: early, night and late shifts. I accepted the job without much hesitation because it meant a better life for us.

Oh, the shift patterns were difficult travel-wise because if it was a late shift, finishing around 23.00, or a night shift, starting at 23.00, I was travelling at night, from one town to another on public transport – train and bus – combined with a long walk to and from home. Summer months were fine, but winters weren't that brilliant, because of the weather and having to travel on my own. Looking back on it, I do marvel how I just did it. Well, it had to be done, so I did it. The motivation was always to have a better life for us three.

Luckily, a colleague who became a good friend and was also using the public transport, lived nearby so he often accompanied me on these journeys to and from work. Sometimes another colleague who also lived in Luton was kind enough to give us lifts in his car. We used to have some very deep conversations about the meaning of life, the universe and everything, even when we knew the answer was 42 (*The Hitchhiker's Guide to the Galaxy*).

The shift environment was extremely hard work but also so much fun, working in these large, air-conditioned computer halls where mainframe computer consoles whirred away. There were rows of large data disc drives, reel-to-reel tape decks, card readers and large industrial computer printers, printing telephone bills, payslips and the like on continuous stationery, in a cold and a very noisy environment.

Most of my colleagues were men; it was a very male-dominated environment, with a handful of girls. There was one other girl on my shift who took me under her wing. I knuckled down to learn everything I could. I was accepted and looked after by everyone in my immediate team and the wider computer centre colleagues. My managers told me that my determination, my strength, my work ethic and friendly disposition definitely helped me to be part of a very strong team.

It is quite usual for there to be a very strong team spirit and camaraderie when people work shifts. It was the same with ours. They were good times of working well together, socialising outside work, playing rounders in the park before going in to work on a late shift, going dry slope skiing or meeting in a pub. It was also accepted that some of us cooked food and took it in for everyone, especially Indian food, which was very welcome. Guess who cooked it and took it in for a shift of 13 people?

The socialising included going to the West End to watch *The Life of Brian* and Tommy Cooper live on stage. At work we once dressed up in fancy dress on a night shift as there was no one else around. On night shifts, it was a must to play very loud music through the PA (public address) system installed in the computer hall for communicating between the console operator and tape loaders.

It was a hip thing to play very loud music from cassette tapes, either taped from the radio or concerts or bought ones: everything from the Sex Pistols, The Who, Neil Young, Neil Diamond, Peter Frampton, Eric Clapton, Joan Armatrading, Elton John, and the Stranglers to the Bee Gees and Abba. There was an eclectic selection, depending on which shift members were operating the console on the night.

I knew nothing about this kind of music until then, but very quickly learned all about the punk and rock bands and their music. I was brought up on Indian music, so it was kind of a shock to the system, but I quickly got to like most of it. I had no option, given that the same music was played over and over all night. I even attended the Bob Dylan concert at the Blackbushe Aerodrome in Surrey, with a lovely work colleague and her boyfriend. We all piled into her old Mini Cooper car to get there. It was the first time I saw and heard Joan Armatrading, who was one of the supporting acts.

All these experiences also brought new people into my life and some lifelong friendships. They also brought me self-awareness of my character, determination and strength.

If Not Me, Who Then?

Continuing the theme of taking action, a lot of us are prone to hesitation, procrastination and cogitation. Someone I know always used to say that they needed to cogitate before they made a decision or took action. I'm one of these people who has to just get on with it.

I think the women in my family in general have the ability to assimilate information quickly and act on it. I'm referring to major decisions. Of course, there are times when all of us have to think through consequences or work out a plan that may depend on several factors that have to be addressed before the action is taken. This also shows the self-reliance of not giving the power to someone else to decide on our behalf.

My aunt, one of my mum's two younger sisters, married at an early age, in the 1950s. Later, when she'd had four daughters, she decided that she wanted to finish her education. She completed her matriculation (the equivalent of O-levels or high school) before undertaking a teacher training course for four further years to graduate as a teacher. She went on to be the principal of a girl's school in one of the towns of Gujarat, and turned the school around before passing the baton to her third daughter to carry on the good work as principal of the school.

My aunt was a trailblazer, with her passion for girls' education and bettering oneself. Even now, in her late 80s, she keeps showing her passion to better herself, for example by learning yoga from one of her daughters in the last five years. The discipline of doing yoga every morning, going for walks and exercising has kept her so young in mind and body. She puts us younger ones to shame. All her daughters have carved out successful careers, all having the same determination, drive and most of all initiative to be the 'first' in their respective niches.

"If not me, who then?" also applies to life decisions. When I was working for BT, I went on a three-day leadership training course held by BT at one of their training schools in Holborn. I was early and, thinking there wouldn't be anyone there yet, I went into the meeting room, having been informed by the receptionist at the desk that it was OK for me to do so. As I entered the room, I saw that the tables and chairs were arranged in a horseshoe shape and there were name plates of the delegates set out on the tables, in front of the delegates' chairs.

There was one other person sitting there, across the room from the doorway, smoking a cigar and reading *The Times*. He looked up, as I noticed his mop of curly, fair hair and green eyes. He nodded to me and went back to reading his newspaper. I started looking for my seat and found that it was next to him. I took my seat and was very aware of his presence. He didn't say anything and carried on reading his newspaper until the trainer arrived, followed soon afterwards by the other delegates. I thought he was rather stand-offish. I looked at the name plate in front of him. It said Ian Briggs.

However, by lunchtime, my heart was skipping beats. During the lunch break, I called a close friend of mine who was also a colleague at the computer centre. When she answered, I just said, "I think I've found him." "Found who?" she said. "My man," I said. That was that.

This was a Wednesday. On Friday, everyone went to a nearby pub with the trainer, as was the tradition at the time: Friday lunchtime was pub time. We all were talking about life stuff as you do, and I realised that he was not married or attached. As part of the general conversation he said that a young Indian lady who was working with him at the BT Computer Centre at Heathrow was married by arranged marriage; she was always talking about her extended family and from what he could gather, Indian women in the main were not independent.

There was a spark between us, but I knew very well that he was not going to ask me out or he would take a very long time to pluck up the courage to do so. We all finished that day and went our separate ways. He did not say a word, but I knew. I contacted him a couple of weeks after that and asked him out on a date. We met a month later because we were both working totally different shifts. He admitted that he had been thinking about ways of asking me out, even taking advice from the young Indian lady who worked with him as to how he should approach me. Luckily, I made it easy for him.

We met at St Pancras station where he was waiting for me under the station clock for my train from Luton to arrive. He asked if I'd like to go to Covent Garden. So off we went. When we arrived at Covent Garden, only one of the three lifts to take up the passengers to the street level was working. He said, "Let's use the stairs." That's 193 steps to get to the street level. I did it but they seemed never-ending. I don't like steps. To this day, I have never forgotten what a pain that was. We were about to cross a busy road and due to the traffic, I was hesitant and so he just took my hand, and we were over to the other side. That was an electrifying moment. I was totally smitten, and so the rest of the first date went well.

Although it seemed just natural for both of us, there were not that many young Indian women dating English men, not in the 1980s. It was always funny to watch some people's reactions when they saw us walking hand in hand, even in London. Often, they'd just stare. Luckily, no one said anything because I don't think he would have taken it lightly.

Exactly a year after our first date, he called me from a coin-operated telephone box, (one of those famous red telephone boxes), as his mum and dad were staying with him at the time. I was expecting the call and knew what he may be saying. Just as he was about to propose, the telephone ran out of money and so it started beeping for more coins. So funny. He quickly put some more money in the slot and finished proposing. I of course had to say yes after all that money he'd put in the telephone box.

It was a different ball game to tell my mum about him, that we planned to get married with her blessings. My sister knew, and Mum had an inkling that I was seeing someone but I hadn't said anything. It wasn't the done thing at the time. Mum wasn't happy when I did tell her that I wanted to get married. Mum was shocked as she had always thought that I would marry a nice Indian man.

To be honest, I was not looking to get married; it just happened that we fell in love. I had never thought that I would be marrying an English man either; I had dreams of marrying a dashing, dark

Indian prince who would sweep me off my feet to his palatial kingdom, just as all young Indian girls dreamed of at the time when I was young.

The atmosphere was very strained between Mum and me for a week or so. In the end, I told Mum that she had two options: either to give me her blessing to marry the man I wanted to marry, or never again mention to me my getting married. I did not want a parade of nice Indian boys and their families coming to see me as a viable prospect. I was serious about it so after a couple of days, Mum said I should ask him to come over to meet her.

So, he came to meet Mum. He was very charming and Mum was civil to him. She asked him if he loved me. He said yes. She told him in no uncertain terms that he'd better look after me or else. She would not stand for any nonsense from him because he was a very lucky man to have met me and for me to have fallen in love with him. Straight-talking as ever, that was my mum. Suffice to say, we had Mum's blessing to get married.

The wedding was a two-day affair, simplified as we didn't really have the money. It was a different kind of wedding as we had the civil ceremony at the local register office on one day and the Indian wedding on the next, both very cold November days. It snowed on the morning of the Indian wedding. We did everything that we could ourselves, nothing like the grand Indian weddings of today where £100k gives you just a normal wedding. We invited all the people from my work, families and friends. Most of the wedding guests were from my side. Ian's brother and family and his best friend and best friend's wife were there.

The message here is to just make it happen. If it's your happiness at stake, your career, ambition, life goals, then just do it. It may take a while, but it will happen.

Thinking Differently

Anyone with a career or in business over the past couple of decades will have heard a lot of buzzwords being bandied around, such as 'thinking outside the box' or being creative, being unconventional or just being resourceful. I feel that I have been unconventional and resourceful most of my life.

One of the lessons in life has been that as long as I am not hurting anyone and being honest and true to myself, without breaking any laws, then, if it calls for being unconventional, so be it.

Looking back, there have been numerous occasions when I have taken the plunge, done what seemed right at the time. Most of my life has been such. Has that helped me? I'd say yes. Did I think I was doing anything different? Not really.

I feel that all of us have the ability to think differently. Not being average or doing things that everyone else is doing. Sometimes I wonder what my life would have been like if it had been normal, if I'd done all the average things people do through their lives, such as completing my education, having a normal family, being married traditionally, having kids and retiring. Then I wake up and realise that it wasn't for me anyway; I wouldn't have survived in a traditional life.

Organisations are always looking for new talent, people who think differently and use their initiative to find new ways to solve problems or bring in new business. In my career at BT, towards the latter years of the computer age in the late 1980s and early 1990s, the company started using assessment centres for recruiting computer operations staff in different areas. The assessment process took about a day to run, with the candidates being called in groups of anything up to 20 people at a time.

They were set different exercises, tasks and activities, either as individuals or in groups. My job was to run these assessments in conjunction with senior managers and directors, looking for the right-fit candidates in terms of their interaction with others, team spirit, attitude, personality and behaviour. One can train an individual in new skills, but not in their attitude and their interactions with others. These assessment centres worked well to recruit people who thought differently.

It was a pleasure to introduce a similar concept in my later career at the airport. I used this system for many years, for all sorts of roles and levels. In the beginning, some of the managers were sceptical about the process and of the results, until they experienced it themselves as assessors. Often the candidates were doubtful about what we were trying to do. They couldn't see the relevance of applying for a job as a plumber or an electrician and going through an assessment centre.

At the end of the session, every time, most people said how impressed they were with it all. How it all worked so well and that they could see straight away the reasons why I was running these selection processes to get the right people in the organisation. It worked during my tenure and it was so rewarding to see most of the people I had recruited flourish and progress to bigger and better things, including directorships of international airports.

These processes are designed to be open-minded and to give everyone involved a chance to succeed. In life it's the same; being open-minded has given me the opportunities to truly discover uncharted waters, as it were.

Some of the best outcomes I've had from being open-minded have related to the people it has brought into my life. The lifelong friendships blossomed from weird and wonderful beginnings. For example, Twitter. Twitter as a social media platform is something that either you 'get' and love – or you don't.

When my business partner at that time and I started the HR consultancy business, a business coach told us that Twitter was the one thing we should get involved in, that we should establish the company's presence on it. I loved it from the beginning and still do. In Twitter's heyday, there were tweetups: organised, in-person gatherings of Twitter users with common interests. Some friendships blossomed from these; others unfortunately quietly withered.

Two of my special friends – Jayne and Lizzy – came into my life through such a gathering. Once again, I was keeping an open mind, when I met Jayne at someone's book launch in Milton Keynes. We looked at each other and realised that we had exchanged tweets. The thing was, if you liked the look of them and if there was some synergy in your work, you arranged to have a coffee. Well, that's still the way people do business now.

Jayne and I now look back and laugh about the way it happened at that first proper coffee meeting. We'd arranged and rearranged the dates to meet and I think after chasing her for some dates, we eventually met after about three attempts. As she worked from home, I said I would travel up to her. Jayne was not so sure about me; after all, there didn't seem to be much in common with me, an Indian lady of more advanced years than her, doing HR when she was into all sorts of coaching and other exciting aspects of work. I arrived at her house on a cold, rainy day. We went into her garden office and started chatting – politely.

The conversation started about the normal mundane stuff that we talk about, like the weather and the travel and, "Tell me about what you actually do in your HR work. What did you do before that?" and so on. Somehow, the conversation turned to losing family members and how it had affected both of us. Suddenly we started talking about her having lost her dad very recently and me, my mum.

Oh, my goodness, the floodgates opened. Instead of a 30-minute chat, I was there for nearly three hours. We couldn't stop talking. I still tease her that I could read on her face when I first arrived, "Why did I say I would meet her, this Indian lady at my home, we have nothing really in common. I'll be polite and get rid of her in half an hour."

The other friend, Lizzy, and I couldn't be more different in our backgrounds if you tried. Again, we met through the Twitter club and just gelled so quickly. The three of us have become great friends, with a friendship very much of the no-holds-barred variety. More about it a bit later.

Dare to Dream

We all have dreams, no matter who we are. Even when life is so hard that you think it doesn't allow you the luxury of dreaming, somewhere, a ray of sunshine, through a chink suddenly gives one the hope, the audacity to dream. Mum, my sister and I, we all have had dreams.

Over the years, we looked at life as a gift. Bit by bit, we dreamed of being better than we were, of having beautiful clothes, shoes, good food on the table, being able to spend money on luxuries, the freedom to buy something on impulse.

Once we were able to afford a decent lifestyle, it was amazing how Mum once again made money go a long way. She made beautiful clothes from yards and yards of material bought at the local market stalls or from fabric shops. She loved knitting beautiful jumpers and cardigans for friends and family members, so it was her way of being able to have the freedom to choose what she wanted to spend the money on. She and I would go to the local Saturday markets in neighbouring towns and come away with these yards of fabric.

This was also the time when we had told Mum not to spend any money on any of us, but to spend it on herself. Suddenly Mum had the best time shopping. We would visit her favourite shops, such as M&S, Debenhams, Littlewoods and Evans to buy trousers, tops, cardigans and shoes. Hush Puppies were her favourite shoes. Mum had swollen feet, very swollen, so her shoes had to be wide fitting and soft. Anyway, if she liked the fitting of a pair of trousers, that was it; she'd buy all the colours she could find in that style. The same went for the cardigans, the shoes, the long tops – it was all bought in bulk.

When Mum used to visit India, from the early 1980s until 2002, our family loved her for the shopping she did. They used to love taking her shopping because it was a great show. Mum would always buy colourful saris and blouses of every shade of every colour imaginable. One of the last times she was in India, around 2000, she had decided that she was going to buy very expensive silk saris, at least seven or eight, or maybe more if she found any interesting ones.

Well, my cousin, aunt, cousin's wife and my sister-in-law took her to one of these exclusive places. The family remembers even to this day how much fun they all had. Mum was buying saris, each of them costing between 20,000 and 25,000 rupees, a lot of money in those days. Even now, after 20 years, it can buy you a very decent silk sari. I think she bought seven or eight in the end. The shopkeeper was so happy; everyone was happy.

In India, the shopkeeper always asks you for your address or contact details to inform you of future promotions and deals. My cousin gave his address, so for a number of years afterwards, they kept getting promotional leaflets from this exclusive shop. I still have these saris, bar one. That's a story for later, an interesting one too; that was so typical of Mum.

Ian and I were fortunate enough to dream of luxuries and be able to afford them. One of those memorable occasions was one Christmas when we were going south to my sister and brother-in-law's home. Mum was staying with me at the time. Hubby and I were both working at the airport. He was an operations manager, in charge of car parks and buses. He always went in on Christmas Day to wish the staff on duty a merry Christmas.

The chief executive of the airport was famous for this too. He was the best chief executive I have ever worked for in my career. Everyone at the airport respected and admired him. He would travel from London on Christmas Day, visit every single department at the airport, making sure everyone was OK. All the staff on duty were bought Christmas lunches before he travelled back to London.

On this particular Christmas Day, Ian said he was going to pop up to the airport to wish his team members who were on duty merry Christmas and that he wouldn't be long. I reminded him not to take too much time. After a while he called me from the airport to say that he was going to be a bit delayed so Mum and I should drive down to my sister's and he'd follow soon. I was very confused and couldn't understand why he was going to take so long. I was livid. So Mum and I travelled to my sister's home in my car. Anyway, we arrived, and hubby arrived soon afterwards. When it was time to open all the presents, I was still seething. The last thing I was given was a black plastic bucket by hubby.

I was in no mood for any silly games. There was a small parcel inside the bucket. I opened the parcel, which contained a sponge and a bottle of car shampoo. There was another small parcel inside. I opened it and to my surprise it a had a badge of a Porsche on the key fob and a key. Ian had driven the white 944 down south from Luton. He had bought the car and hidden it in one of the airport car parks a few weeks before Christmas.

Apparently, everyone at work knew about it except me. The family were all in on it too. On that day, when Ian was driving the car from the airport car park to my sister's, the motorway was practically empty. The airport chief executive was going back to London after his Christmas round, and passed hubby on the motorway, waving and smiling at Ian, giving him the thumbs-up sign, very happy about the Porsche, my surprise Christmas gift.

Daring to dream also means being able to welcome successes with open arms and heart. It also means being grateful and accepting all gifts coming our way with humbleness. Mum was always one to shower people with gifts and equally happy to receive them gratefully. One of the most precious gifts Mum received was the honour of being a community leader. Once again, she broke the mould of doing something differently.

The community we belong to in Luton, the Brahmin Association of Luton, honoured Mum not once but twice for her guidance, leadership and her contribution to the services for the betterment of the community. She was the first lady honoured in the association by draping a shawl over her shoulders. It is usually a woollen Indian Kashmir beige or stone coloured long shawl, with the edges embroidered in a typical pattern used to honour men, community leaders. As you can imagine, it was a very humbling and proud honour for Mum and for the family.

I had these two shawls in the wardrobe, intact. In 2019, there were two occasions when they were the right gifts for two lovely ladies who in their own way have been a pillar of their society for their relentless work; most importantly they have been part of my world. One of the ladies, who is a professional in the HR world, very well-known and respected in London and in the HR global world for her selfless contribution to many charities, was given the Freedom of the City; I was one of the fortunate ones invited to the ceremony.

I had no idea what suitable gift I should buy this special friend when it suddenly dawned on me that I should give her one of Mum's shawls. When I gave the gift to my friend, she was totally taken aback, very emotional that I was giving such a treasure to her. I was so happy, knowing that she'd cherish it all her life, the shawl befitting the two honoured ladies.

I gave the second shawl to our dear friend Pilar's mum in Spain, my Spanish family. The whole family loved Mum and called her 'Mummy', just as we did. When I presented her with the shawl, Pilar translated from English to Spanish about how Mum had been honoured with this shawl and I wanted her to have it. She just hugged me, hugged the shawl, sitting there crying her eyes out from pure joy and love. Even writing about it makes me misty-eyed. It was such an emotional July evening in Spain.

Daring to dream means welcoming success, joy and intellectual personal growth; being bold enough to expect and humble enough to accept it every time.

Well, I am no longer dreaming. Life is good.

Chapter 7

You Are Loveable

Self-Confidence

Women are more likely than men to have confidence issues. I think that men are perhaps much better at hiding their self-doubts, or perhaps women find themselves in ever-decreasing circles of fulfilling self-prophesy of lack of confidence.

My experience as a woman of lack of self-confidence came from being told or made to feel that I was not good enough. I don't have these feelings that often now. I have realised over the years that I can't please everyone every time, all the time. I can't be friends with everyone, or as hubby often tells me when I've been let down, that I expect everyone to be my friend because I think they are.

I'm giving people a place in my heart and unless they prove otherwise, they are a friend. Unfortunately, that doesn't follow. Not everyone sees me like that. I'm learning a bit at a time. I still tend to take everyone I meet at face value, seeing them as good people who will reciprocate my open-armed open-hearted friendship attitude.

One of the places where this happened to me was in a job I took on and loved from the very beginning. The people in the department were all women, wary of my being there, especially as I was more qualified than anyone there and the first Indian woman in the department. During my probationary period in this permanent role, it became evident that jealousies were playing a big part in trying to keep me down, in fact to push me out, because I was different.

The manager told me of how the managers and directors of the company loved me, but that some of the members of the team did not, jeopardising the chance of my position becoming permanent at the end of the six-month probationary period. I just worked on what I had to do to win them over. It was a case of understanding what it was that they didn't like about me, what they feared about me and, without making any waves or treading on anyone's toes, carrying on being effective in my work, the progress that I had set my heart on, and slowly being accepted by the team. I did win them over, most of them, becoming lifelong friends with some, and I went on to have a great career there for over 17 years.

One of the life lessons I've learned is, "Just because someone didn't love you the way you loved them doesn't mean that you are not loveable." It does not have to be sexual; it is all about the confidence within ourselves of being loved for who we are. In the past, when I thought about fitting into an acceptable mould of normality, I realised that I couldn't because, to start with, I was the wrong colour.

To be honest, colour has not been an issue for me. I can count on one hand the number of times someone has treated me badly, openly, because of the colour of my skin. I love my colour and in fact often my friends say they wish they were my colour and that they tanned as easily as I do.

Yes, I do go dark, very dark in summer if I stay out a long time in the sun. I have often been asked whether I really tan by those who didn't think that dark-skinned people tanned. I love the sun but cannot stay in it for too long. I have become one of those people who like the weather to be just so, ambient, around 26°C to 27°C, not too cold, not too warm, just right to walk around in summer clothes without thinking of taking a shawl or cardigan with me.

Self-confidence comes with knowing who you are and feeling comfortable with your self-image. Given that I was generally the first Asian Indian to be in the places where I have been in my life, that's how it was and has been. The first Indian in an airline company data processing unit, first one to be on shift in a computer centre, the first Indian head of HR for an airport and perhaps the first Indian HR consultant in Luton. My cultural difference made me different and interesting; I have accepted that I am different, which is an advantage

Lack of self-confidence or lack of self-esteem tends to stem from a number of different circumstances, such as always being criticised during one's childhood or in the home environment, which is not conducive to promoting confidence. My childhood was such that it didn't give me the nurturing that every child deserves. Despite that, with God's grace, thankfully, I think I have turned out OK as a human being. I have my mum to thank for being that constant voice of encouragement. She was never a demonstrator of her feelings or love in the way other mothers would. She just was supportive and there every step of the way for my sister and me.

My message here is to embrace our individuality and have the confidence of being loveable. It starts by acknowledging our individuality in every way. In fact, it has worked in my favour all along in the UK, or wherever I have gone, because of the way I dress in flamboyant colours, as my mum did, wearing with pride Indian saris and suits on religious festivals, community functions and even at general functions. If it's a formal occasion that requires being dressed up in a long dress or a cocktail dress, I tend to wear my Indian outfits. I love Indian outfits and saris and just like Mum, I have kept up the tradition of buying silk saris every year when I'm visiting India. All that speaks volumes about my self-confidence and individuality.

At work, because of my company branding in orange, black and white, over the years, I have developed my own style of wearing an orange scarf or shawl, which has become part of my professional image. I often receive orange shawls or scarves as presents from family and friends and even business friends. My business friends now ask me where my orange scarf is if I'm not wearing one.

Inner Knowledge

Inner knowledge is that certainty in ourselves that gives us the confidence to be what we are, who we are and choose how we conduct ourselves with others. Often, I just know, no explanation as to how, I just do. It becomes very interesting when this happens in conversations with friends, family members or business clients. I say something and they say, "You're right Bina," and I say, "Yes, I know." It's just a fact and a statement. Often, friends will wind me up about it or chunter on about how I'm always right (actually, not always, but most of the time).

That inner knowledge is also a reflection of your character, inner beauty, attitude, personality, grace and kindness.

My mum's eldest sister was a graceful lady, beautiful and kind. She was respected by all Mum's family. She was second born of ten siblings: five brothers and five sisters. She was called *Motiben*, meaning elder sister, by the siblings and their other halves. My aunt ran the household expertly. Everyone looked up to her for advice and guidance.

I remember first meeting her a few days before my seventh birthday. We had arrived in Mumbai and were staying at my aunt's place. Travelling from Kampala, it was quite a journey by rail and some nine days of crossing the Indian Ocean from Mombasa, Kenya to Mumbai, in a huge liner, a steamer as we called it at the time. This whole trip in India lasted nearly five months; I think it was one big adventure at that age.

Everything was a new experience to me, including the sea voyage, our cabin, the food and the entertainment for kids on board. I nearly fell into the sea when I tripped while coming down some steps, but luckily was caught by a person coming up the steps. More of the new experiences of meeting all this family that I knew about but hadn't thought about – oh, and having my tonsils out in a private clinic situated on the famous Marine Drive in Mumbai.

Having my tonsils out meant that I could have as much ice cream as I wanted. I remember ice cream being made at home by my aunt's four sons, who were all a lot older than I – my cousin brothers. I loved them all straight away as they took it in turn to look after me, entertain me and take me out for drives.

From that first trip to India, my aunt had won over my heart too and all through her life, she was more than a mother figure, a shining example of a matriarch with a kind heart. Some 12 years after my first trip to India, I travelled to Bombay, as it was at the time, yet again on a new experience, this time of being a college student.

My main base was at my aunt and uncle's place in their huge three-storey bungalow, which had seen better days since being built in the 1930s. I moved to a hostel for girls from abroad, mainly girls from the East African countries, to be near my college. It was still a long journey across the city by train and a long walk either end.

Well, here again, I became friends with other students who had arrived from Kenya: my roommates to be precise. I'm pleased to say all through the decades, throughout our lives, we have remained friends. We often reminisce about those carefree days of midnight feasts of potato crisps and Coca-Cola, going to the Marine Drive or the Juhu beach to eat tasty Indian street food and fast food such as *bhel puri*, *pani puri*, *dosas* and *chaat* – we just ate and ate.

There were boys too. Luckily, at that point I wasn't interested in boys because I was in India for a purpose: to study so that after graduation, I could get a job and take Mum and my sister, who were back in Kampala, away from it all. Meanwhile I had some freedom, a respite from everything.

All through my time there as a student of microbiology, which I did not finish as my father had other ideas, my aunt became my mum, my guardian, one of my role models. I always remember how she managed the complexities of life in Bombay in the late 1960s and early 1970s, and how everything was done meticulously, on time, to meet the three grown-up sons' schedules, my uncle's schedule and her stepmother-in-law's schedule. By this time, her eldest son, my cousin brother number 1, and cousin brother 2 were married and had young children. Cousin brother 1 lived separately nearby.

My aunt knew that she was respected and that she had the status of being an elder in the family with a voice of reason. She had been brought up by my grandmother, her mother, another strong lady who was loved and respected by everyone in the family and community.

Let It Be Love

Although I have covered a few times the aspects of our feeling, our love for ourselves, it is so difficult to be kind to ourselves. We all see and hear it in the media, in magazines and in wellbeing programmes that you should be kind to yourself. What does that mean? To love yourself, to put yourself before everyone else.

Kindness to me goes hand in hand with love. When you feel love towards another human being, for whatever reason, in whatever measure, that's when kindness happens. That natural progression of feeling to look after someone, extend a hand of support, show empathy, show that you care.

In the same way, kindness and love go hand in hand for oneself. We don't think consciously about whether we are being kind to ourselves or say aloud to ourselves, "I'm going to be kind to you now." It just means that we look after ourselves just as we would if it was someone else that we were thinking about.

As I have got older, I have become calmer and more in tune with myself. I suppose that I'm kinder to myself. I don't have to prove anything to anyone except myself. By being calmer, and kinder to myself, I don't struggle on my own. I don't feel obliged to prove to the world or to myself that I'm a superwoman. To me, it's all about balance now. By doing so, what has happened is that I am more aware of others' kindness and love towards me, be that from friends, family, business connections or acquaintances.

Allow oneself to be loved. Such a small sentence with such a great meaning. People often put up barriers to being loved, for fear of being hurt, or sometimes they are not even aware that they are being aloof.

Love is the one feeling that one can never have enough of. I have been very lucky, throughout my life, to have people who love me, are kind to me. Mum was lucky to have a such a vast family who loved her for who she was. When she left work in 1981, it was after being laid off by her company as it was moving the dress making factory to Wales, Mum was able to visit India on an open-ended airline ticket for up to a year each time.

She used to stay with all her siblings and their families in turn, loving their company, making up for lost time. There were the long hours of just reminiscing, chatting, playing cards, listening to music and visiting temples all over India or any places of interest. She enjoyed being part of the family life that she had missed for the previous 40 or so years.

Luckily, it has been equally wonderful for me to visit my extended family regularly. There is no question of staying in a hotel; wouldn't even dream of it. I can visit only for a few weeks each time and so it's a pilgrimage, as it were, a whistle-stop tour of about three or four main cities in Gujarat and Maharashtra states, sometimes to

Bangalore. Each time it's just being with the elders, my aunts and uncles and their growing families. Some of them now have their fourth generation great-grandkids.

My British friends ask me about my visits to India. They want to know all that happens there because they know about my huge extended family in India and how much they love me, and I love them. I tell them that I just need to worry about travelling from our home to Heathrow airport and then to the arrivals hall in Mumbai. Once I'm out of the airport, everything's taken care of as one of the brothers will be there waiting for me outside the arrivals hall.

From that point, until I return to the doors of the departures area at the airport after my holiday in India, I don't have to worry about anything. Everything works like clockwork, all planned on my Excel spreadsheet scheduling, right down to half-days of where I will be, with whom and what we'll be doing. The Excel spreadsheet schedule is then emailed out to everyone. I'm treated like royalty there. In our Indian culture, there is a saying that when a married woman goes to her maternal home, especially to her mother's family, she is treated like royalty.

In the olden days and even now, in some extended families in India, a married woman works hard all day, with not much respite and sometimes not that much support from the extended family members. So, on any planned holiday to visit her maternal home, it's a real holiday as she is given the rest she needs. The maternal family is addressed as *mosad* and truly, I don't do a thing, I'm not allowed to do anything for the whole time I'm at my *mosad*.

I'm also very lucky with the friends in Spain and Poland, because they all treat hubby and me like royalty. In fact, one of the friends in Poland said to me that her mum makes sure that everything is to my liking because I am their Queen visiting them, honestly. It is so heart-warming; love them to bits.

I'm so grateful to have such wonderful people in my life. When I'm in Poland with my family of 5Ms – they all have their Christian names starting with the letter M – I love that we have all the speciality fare: lots of vegetarian dishes; made especially for me and there is always the tradition of having our Saturday dinner at the famous Indian restaurant in the city. M3 used to work at the airport in Luton and became a great friend to Ian and me; when she returned home to Poland, the friendship carried on being stronger by the day.

I Have Legs!

While I was growing up in Kampala, the standard mode of dressing was skirt and blouse for school, dress at home and sometimes dressed up in an Indian suit or a sari. When I turned 13, my dad decided that I should not show my arms or legs. Given that it's a warm country, people did wear sleeveless tops and blouses.

I was also forbidden to wear skirts or dresses; I wasn't allowed to show my legs. So, I donned an Indian trouser suit of kameez and salwar. I felt awful, but that's how it was. I remember sandals with small, pointed heels being the height of the fashion. I bought these beautiful strappy sandals: slingbacks. I loved them.

I wore them once and that was it; I was not allowed to wear them because they had heels and were fashionable. I had to pull off the heels, so the sandals were flat, but of course the way they were made, they were not meant to lie flat on the ground. Never wore them again. Even when I was studying in India, there were strict instructions from my father to my aunt in Bombay about what I was allowed to do and wear, and who I could mix with.

Well, as you can imagine, I grew up feeling bad about my body. The message was loud and clear, that I was not good enough. My body was not good enough to be seen, not even my arms. It's not that I wanted to flaunt my body; I just wanted to be able to wear normal clothes like everyone else. Not only that, my father never complimented us on anything, so once again, we felt worthless. I always thought I was ugly.

Once in the UK, we were able to wear what we wanted. I was so conditioned to not showing my body that it took a while to wear dresses or to show my arms and legs. I never liked my legs because I was always given the impression that they were not attractive enough until one day a friend, looking at some of my pictures from decades ago remarked that I had legs.

I was totally taken aback. I asked him again about it and he said, "Yes, you have legs." I had never ever thought that I had 'legs!' Apparently, I still have 'legs!' So, there you go, it's never too late to be told that you have 'legs'. Suddenly, looking back at my pictures over the last few decades, I realised that I wasn't that bad looking after all. Maybe in some pictures, when people said I looked pretty, I was pretty. Hey, there's hope for me after all. Life's looking rosier by the minute.

There is a beautiful picture of my mum when she was young, soon after she was married, probably at 16 or 17 at the most. She had very long hair which she used to braid into two plaits. I never remember seeing her like that from the time I got to recognise and remember her. She was a beauty.

Recently, I saw Peanuts strip with the caption of Lucy saying, "I just want to be a raving cutie!" It was a kindred spirit saying it. I posted it on Instagram and had the comment back that I am. How kind!

Chapter 8

You Will Attract the Right People (the Ones Who Matter)

Shared Interests

I often wonder how I've met some of the most amazing people in this world. Everyone has a story, but we don't realise that until we start speaking to them. I find connecting with people fairly easy, especially if there are shared interests, don't you?

Music connects the world over and so it was no different with me. I was brought up on Indian film music, now known as Bollywood music, and Gujarati traditional and religious songs and hymns called *bhajans*, which are the foundation of many get-togethers to this day in the UK and anywhere in the world when Hindus meet. The get-together is also known as a *satsang*, meaning spiritual gathering.

In Luton, there are a number of these community groups that meet regularly, all run by volunteers. One such group, called Bhajan Bhojan, which means devotional songs and dinner, has been going strong for the last 19 years. Mum and I visited it a couple of times when she was in fairly good health, probably in early 2002. The group is run jointly by two associations, the Brahmin Association and Lohana Samaj, both for Hindu castes, Brahmin and Lohana. The event is held from 1.30pm to 6.30pm on the first Sunday of every month in a local Catholic church hall. It's a free event and all are welcome. It's held in a sacred place regardless of the religious denomination of that place.

There is usually an Indian music group, musicians and singers, all amateurs. Some have attained Indian classical music training over the years, giving up their time for the community. The singing finishes around 5pm, after which there is a full Indian meal, normally sponsored by someone in the name of their dear departed or often as a celebration of someone's success, a wedding, or a new born child: all life events are celebrated here.

After Mum died, the trustees of the Brahmin Association, who have all known our family for the last 40 years, took me under their wing. They kept asking me to attend because it would help me to be among friends and in a spiritual environment. After a while, I gave in and attended in 2004 and to this day I have never looked back. It is one event that I look forward to every first Sunday of the month; it's sacred to me. The singing, the people, the music, the harmony, the energy and vibes that it creates, is indescribable. It binds us all.

The age range of the congregation can be anything from a few months old to 90. We have the regulars as well as many visitors who come from all over the UK. The environment is that of celebration of life in oneness. Children are encouraged to participate and sing, play musical instruments and help in any way they can. It's been an absolute joy to see so many of the youngsters grow up over the last 16 years into young adults, having brilliant careers, extremely well mannered, talented musicians and singers. A lot of the attendees have become good friends, so the boundaries have merged between social and religious links.

Bollywood – as it has been known for decades – is another common interest that binds all Indians together for its music, grand film stars, heroes and heroines. Indians love the cinema and so I too was brought up on a diet of popular Indian cinema and its music. I remember at a tender age of perhaps four or five knowing the names of all the popular actors and actresses. I knew the names of 'playback singers', such as Lata Mangeshkar, Mohammed Rafi, Asha Bhosle and many more evergreen singers, such as Kishore Kumar, Manna Dey and Mukesh, to name a few who have all left their rich legacies of Indian music.

It was quite common for my grown-up cousins on my paternal side in Kampala to take me down to the cinema houses to look at the billboards of the films being shown at the time so that I could identify the stars of the films for them. My love of Indian music hasn't died, but has faded a bit as I have been a little out of touch with it. I still love the music from the golden eras of a few decades ago. Indian mainstream music has changed over the years, though funnily enough several young singers are still attracted to the traditional devotional and classical Indian music, so once again, we are given an opportunity to listen to some wonderful young talent singing much-loved songs.

My family in India all love music and have such beautiful singing voices. Every time I visit, we all end up playing a musical parlour game called *Antakshari* meaning the last letter of the final word. Basically, two teams play the game against each other. One starts the competition by singing a few lines of a song. The last letter of the last word of the last line becomes the first letter of the first word of the first line of the song that the opposing team has to sing. Everyone joins in the singing. Such fun, as each team tries to end their song with a difficult final letter of the final word of their final line. Lots of laughing and good-humoured bantering goes on.

When shared interests draw people together, it does not matter who you are or what background you come from; all that brings you together is the joy of sharing something special. Once again, you'll agree that music of different kinds bring us together, bringing us all love and joy from being with people that we love. You just have to look at the faces around you and you know.

In the 70s and 80s I started to love English music, mainly the romantic ballads, the gentler sounds of Barbra Streisand, Diana Ross, Motown, to name a few. Around Christmas 2018, Ian found out that that a Barbra Streisand concert was being held the following summer in Hyde Park in London. Hubby managed to get us some tickets, so we and our friend Berni, who had flown in from Poland to be at the concert, arrived in Hyde Park on a cool July evening as we hadn't wanted to be there all day. The gates had opened around lunchtime.

The place was a tad busy, with some 65,000 concert-goers! We found a patch of grass to sit down on and even though the stage seemed to be a million miles away from us, we had managed to be near a couple of the giant Diamond Vision screens. There was a mass picnic atmosphere to watch Barbra Streisand at 77 and still clearly at the peak of her powers – the lady gave a great performance. The razzmatazz of it all; I just loved her. There were a lot more women there than men, but it was wonderful to hear the men singing away too.

One of the best memories of that night was when the concert finished at around 11pm. Everyone was being directed through regulated exit gates, one being by Marble Arch tube station. As the concert-goers were walking down the road, in the middle of the road even, everyone was singing away in harmony, with one voice, all smiling away.

We had to walk further down to the next station, Bond Street, and as we headed down the underground passageways, slowly making our way to the trains, all we could hear was *Memories* being sung in true harmony and in unison. You can just imagine, can't you, like any concert-goers, when they've been together, experiencing the music they love, the barriers disappear and everyone shares those moments together – be they teenagers or people of more advanced years. We all love singing along with our favourite music. That evening certainly etched a lot of wonderful memories on our minds and in our hearts that will stay there for a long time.

For something completely different, I can say with certainty that we have eclectic tastes in people, places and music. For example,

Berni introduced us to Polish jazz and in particular the talents of one of Poland's leading jazz pianists – Leszek Możdżer. A favourite memory is of a trip we made to London in 2017 to see him, Swedish bassist Lars Danielsson and Israeli percussionist Zohar Fresco perform at Ronnie Scott's as part of the club's Piano Trio Festival that year. Amazing talent – all of them – and a demonstration that music, and the love of it, knows no borders. As it happens, a long-postponed trip (thanks to the pandemic) to see Możdżer, Danielsson and Fresco perform live again, this time in Warsaw, is planned for spring 2021. We shall see.

It's so true that we make music with the right people in our lives. Music makes memories and keeps those memories alive. Life would be so boring without music, don't you think?

Life is a Fun Journey

I have come a long way from my roots and looking back on it, it's been a good life in the main. Some people are not this lucky to have experienced all the good things I have and, most importantly, the people whom I have been fortunate to meet along the way. Most have stayed and I have been able to call them friends. The variety and differences in nationalities, cultures and background have brought a rich mixture of personalities and experiences to my world. Lots of fun and friendships.

A friend recently remarked that I have had so many wonderful experiences in life, there's clearly plenty of content for my book. Once again, I was surprised that friends think I have lots of wonderful experiences. I think everyone does; it's just that some like me talk about them more than others.

In addition, Ian's love of watching motor racing, photography and cycling has taken us travelling quite a bit in Europe and America, though there's plenty more to see yet. In 1984, Ian and I went to the 24 Hours of Le Mans motor race for the first time. We went on an organised coach tour for a long weekend from early Friday morning to Tuesday evening. The coach went from London Victoria to Dover, on a ferry to Calais and across northern France down through Paris and on to Le Mans. We stayed on the coach for the whole time in one of the car parks reserved for coaches at the circuit, the Red Car Park or Parking Rouge. We met a young couple on the coach who became great friends from there on, having a common interest of motor racing and Le Mans.

During the daytime, it wasn't so bad as it was a warm June, weather for wearing shorts. We enjoyed the start of the race, walking around the circuit to different vantage points of watching the race, going to the 'village' where all the eateries and stalls selling racing merchandise were and having a walk around the fun fair as well. Once it got to around 10pm, however, we girls were ready for sleep.

We went back to the coach. The men freshened up and off they went for most of the night to watch the race. The temperature plummeted through the night, so oh my goodness, it was one of the most uncomfortable nights I've ever spent away from home – trying to sleep on a coach seat surrounded by other weary, snoring motor racing fans.

We loved the race, the atmosphere and the whole experience of Le Mans including the absolutely beautiful cars on and off the circuit, Porsches being our favourite. We especially loved seeing people parading around the city, the circuit and the public areas in their prized classic and vintage cars, which had all been brought out for the week. It was basically like attending a week-long classic car show. As for the race itself well, that would take a whole book to describe it, just wonderful.

We travelled to Le Mans for the race another 18 times, driving down to the circuit, the car loaded for a two-week holiday. One week in Le Mans and the following week, elsewhere in France, discovering most of the *départements* (regions) during those holidays. One of those drives took us through a small village called Binas. And of course, we had to take a picture of Bina standing next to the village sign Binas – as you do.

After two years of trying different places to stay for the race, we were lucky to find a beautiful *chambre hôte* (bed and breakfast) in a hamlet setting in a suburb of Le Mans, about 7km from the circuit, owned by a wonderful couple, Robert and Lucette.

They were farmers with a huge vegetable farm up the lane that produced all sorts of crops that were sold to restaurants in Paris. We didn't speak much French and they didn't speak much English but over the years Madame, as we called Lucette, was so friendly and welcoming. We had our franglais and a sign language of gestures to get us by; armed with the dictionaries in our hands, we held wonderful conversations.

It was a lovely little holding they had with a huge barn, a stream running through an enormous garden with large flower beds, fruit trees, tall plane and fir trees and two houses: one for them and one with four large bedrooms and a communal dining and living area for the guests, all very rustic. Both Monsieur and Madame were born in this little hamlet of French rustic charm. We and the other couple, our friends, became close friends of Madame and Monsieur. Robert's birthday used to be during Le Mans week, so we all used to have champagne and cake on the Sunday evening when we returned from the end of the race.

The whole place was taken over by racegoers for the Le Mans week with people of different nationalities staying there. Over the years, we started to get to know most of the regulars who booked their rooms for the following year as soon as they arrived. We all had our favourite rooms; we were lucky to have the best one in the place. They were such happy times.

Madame used to make her own Calvados and lots of different jams from the fruit produced on the farm. The jams were served at breakfast with all the trimmings of a French breakfast, typically fresh crusty baguettes, cheeses, cold meats, fresh salad tomatoes, orange juice and coffee on tap. When it was time to return home, we were given a bottle of the Calvados and boxes full of jars of the different jams; there was no escape. Most years, I used to share out the beautiful jams with friends and work colleagues, as there was no way we could eat them all in a year.

Two funny incidents come to mind. One was that our friend always insisted on having a barbecue, as the Brits at Le Mans tend to do, regardless of the weather, so he would buy the sausages and burgers from the local hypermarket. On one occasion he bought some burgers that said 'hippo burgers' on the packets, thinking that this meant they were big in size, like jumbo burgers. We looked at the ingredients on the packet just as he was about to cook them, and realised that it said *cheval*, meaning horse. They were burgers made from horse meat. As you can imagine, they were neither cooked nor consumed.

Another time, the same friend bought a whole crate of beer, which on examination of the ingredients turned out to be shandy. The crate stayed in the communal dining area for years after because no one wanted to drink it, even for free. There was a bet every time when we returned to Madame's to see whether the crate had moved or any of the shandy had been drunk or if there were empty bottles. To our delight, the crate of shandy remained untouched. This ritual went on for about four years and it amused us a lot.

Hold on to Your Precious Relationships

People make this world go round for me and as our lovely Barbra Streisand sang, "People who need people are the luckiest people…" People are so precious in our lives and for me, I want to hold on to every single one of them who has brought joy to me.

Often, I find that people aren't valued for who they are until it's too late. This is where I feel I have to be the best I can for that person because they are giving me their best. A lot of great souls in my life have taught me a lesson that I should be the beacon, be the first one to hold out your hand of friendship, the first one to smile a welcome smile and be the best version of yourself. Life is too short to be anything else.

The story of our Spanish family started with one young girl called Pilar, a graduate who came to work for me at the airport in summer months before she went off to do her master's in marketing at Aston University in Birmingham. We kept in touch during her postgraduate year and on her return to work, we became good friends; another waif whom hubby and I took in. Pilar stayed with us while she was looking for suitable rented accommodation.

Pilar's parents were delighted as they said that at least she had her British mum and dad in Luton. Eventually Pilar started working full-time at the airport and over time the relationships blossomed. Pilar's mum and dad came to the UK to visit her and us and they fell in love with my mum, and started calling her 'Mummy' too. Pilar's mum kept hugging my mum and holding her hand during that first visit.

Pilar in the meantime had bought a place with her fiancé in Luton, settling down as young people do. We were there nearby for Pilar. My mum used to say that Pilar was my adopted daughter. At Mum's 70th birthday surprise lunch for all our family and community friends, around 175 people, Pilar dressed up in a beautiful Indian long skirt and tunic top suit, called a *sharara*.

Ian and I visited Pilar's family near Alicante in Spain a year later for a few days leading up to 1 May 2003. It was an emotional visit because by that time Mum was ill and we were waiting for a full report of her prognosis later in the month. The family was so welcoming and once again we were treated royally. Pilar had to be the translator and although we used a Spanish dictionary, she had the hard job right through the visit. We were introduced to all their friends. Pilar's dad sang in a men's traditional choir at Alicante Cathedral, which was truly beautiful. He was a tenor; such a rich voice.

On 1 May, we all walked in the midday heat up this huge hill to the top where there was a small chapel of La Ermita de San Pancracio. It's a famous and popular pilgrimage for Christians in the area. The doors were wide open, and everyone was walking in to take a seat on the handful of benches inside to say their prayers and light a devotional candle. There were lit candles everywhere.

Pilar's mum and I sat down on one of the benches. I have no idea why, it felt so peaceful and yet at the same time, the air was so charged with emotion that I burst into tears. Pilar's mum did too, as I sat there with my hands on my lap, she placed her hands on mine to comfort me. We just sat there for a while. She knew so I did not have to explain anything to her. No words were required.

For the next few years, although the family grew closer for a while, we also drifted apart as I explained earlier in the book, until Pilar was married some seven years later and we received the invitation from her to attend the wedding in a beautiful hotel on the river front in Henley. We did; it was a beautiful ceremony for a beautiful bride and her dark, handsome bridegroom.

After the wedding lunch, one of the last traditional ceremonies in a Spanish wedding is to give the bridal bouquet to a bridesmaid or a matron of honour. Well, in fact, Pilar came over to me and gave me her bridal bouquet. I was unprepared and just blown away by it. I cried, all the women in the family cried, we all cried. It was such a beautiful, loving gesture. Another seven years went by before we once again came together, by which time Pilar had two beautiful children.

I went to visit at their place near Alicante in July 2019, having not seen Pilar for nearly nine years. Pilar had been diagnosed with cancer in 2018. I had to meet her and so I flew over as soon as it was safe for me to do so, mindful of Pilar's fragile health. Pilar and her mum were waiting for me at the airport and as we hugged, the years just melted away.

The visit was a reunion after all those years of having been apart. I spent that long weekend at Pilar's family home in the countryside; she called it a cottage, but it was more like a hacienda. One day at dinner, Pilar's dad started singing a traditional Spanish love song to Pilar's mum. That was so emotional and beautiful.

I call them my Spanish family; such a precious relationship. Time has taught us to value these relationships, the precious bond we have that we nearly gave up on.

Don't Be Afraid to Be You

We all at times feel that we cannot show our true feelings to others, depending on the forum, the people and the circumstances. Not only that, we cannot let people see who we really are. On the other hand, we are bombarded in the media, by gurus and experts to be genuine, to present to the world who we are and be proud of it.

One of the things Mum always used to say was that I had a generous nature but above all, that I was naïve and couldn't lie. I remember the times when I was young that Mum had to instruct me what I could and couldn't say in some circumstances, with other family members or friends in conversation, as I would just be myself and blurt out what was on my mind.

I couldn't understand why I was being asked by Mum to keep quiet about it. Often it would be something like she'd have made a nice Indian sweet and it wasn't ready to be shared or there wasn't enough to go around for all the neighbours and their kids. So, Mum would instruct me not to say anything about the sweets until she was able to offer them to everyone. We'd be at friends or family and Mum would instruct me to eat very little so there was enough to go around – as she knew I had a very big appetite: still do. I love my food.

Over time, this personality trait of being straight and honest about life in general has helped me though. As Mark Twain once said, *"If you tell the truth you don't have to remember anything."*

Being you is also that unique quality that attracts the right people in one's life. I've already said here that so many amazing people have come into my life and have stayed. For instance, the lovely friend Jo who owns and runs a merchandising company. The first few times I met her at business networking events in and around Bedfordshire, I thought she was SO loud. Her laugh, oh my god! You could hear her a mile away when she laughed; she's a great giggler. Sometimes I have to tell her to quieten down. She knows it and then will giggle even more.

We are totally different and yet we have become such close friends, often exchanging messages during the day, sometimes late at night, putting the world to right, but most of all, being there for each other, sharing and supporting. Jo is such a generous-hearted person, a great community supporter to the point that she has always volunteered for good causes and charities, all the time that I have known her over the last eight years.

A great doer, never afraid of hard work, and so creative at the same time, an excellent friend to have. An extremely determined lady; once she sets her mind to do something, she just goes and does it. Recently she set up a Women's Institute group in her village from scratch and not expecting much success at the first meeting, but she signed up around 50 members.

Then there is Lizzy, another one who is a giggler, so mischievous! She reminds me of a young St Trinian's girl with her sense of humour. Lizzy is a gentle soul but knows what she wants and loves her technology. An amazing photographer and artist, she has many talents including collecting lovely handbags and techy stuff. A wonderful soul, even after a personal tragedy of losing a teenage daughter to cancer, she is always smiling and giggling.

I know, when she reads this, she'll just giggle and carry on. Lizzy is a very practical person, so supportive and caring of her family and friends. She is an amazing juggler of her time when it comes to being there for others, especially friends in need of practical as well as emotional support. I love her, most of all for her lovely, infectious, mischievous laugh.

There are so many other wonderful, beautiful souls in my life that I could write a whole book just about them. Suffice to say that I am very grateful for all of them and know that I will keep attracting the right people throughout my life, the ones who matter.

Chapter 9

You Will Always Be True to Yourself

What Makes Me Happy

Happiness is to everyone a different thing, an absolutely personal feeling. Happiness is an inside job, one over which only we have control. For a long time, I never consciously thought about what makes me happy. People, circumstances, places, travelling, feeling loved, valued, sharing love, friendships, things going well and according to plan, sunsets, sunrises, the moon, flowers, cute children, cats, dogs, animals, pictures of nature, the list just goes on and on.

The key is that once I realised what makes me happy, I have made it a priority to be happy. It is an acknowledgement of myself that I have to think of my priorities and that I matter just as much as the people I love. It has become simple to think about my happiness as a must.

People feature a lot in my life. Family and friends do. Friends who become family in a way. Take 5Ms for a start. I briefly mentioned earlier how Ian was friends with one M; he worked with her at the airport. One New Year's Eve we discovered she was on her own, so as we always do, invited M to ours. We had a great time. The following year, M decided to return to Poland, back to her family.

Hubby and I were invited over on an open invitation. We visited in mid-October that year, not knowing the family at all or speaking any Polish. M spoke English of course, and had to become the full-time interpreter for the weekend. Besides, I am very comfortable with dictionaries and hand gestures, so it was not daunting at all. We met 4Ms – mum, dad, brother of M and M herself – all of them having Christian names starting with the letter M. They were so loving and welcoming and soon we felt as though we were very much part of the family.

The friendship continued, and grew stronger as soon we were informed that M was expecting a baby and we were one of the few who knew about it. We were excited when M gave birth to a bonny lass the following year and guess what, the name had to start with the letter M. We all had so many names ready for her, all starting with M! Thus, began the story of 5Ms. They have become our Polish family in every way; we've seen the bonny little baby grow up to be such a lovely young lass, beautiful, talented and most importantly, extremely loving. I became Ciocia Bina (Auntie Bina) from day one – what an honour.

Over the years, we've visited them at least once a year. Holidaying in Spain in the summer months with the 2Ms has become a tradition now, just as has going over to Poland in early December to exchange Christmas presents. We chat every day on WhatsApp as a family group. Buying beautiful dresses and clothes for little M makes me happy. My Polish family make me very happy.

Sunsets and sunrises and full moon nights make me happy, especially the ones over water. When in Spain, going over to the promenade near our apartment and just sitting there quietly watching the sun go down. The Mediterranean sky produces such magnificent sunrises and sunsets. When looking at these miracles in the sky, millions of miles away, I feel as though there's just them and me, when I'm looking up at them, soaking up their splendour. Taking pictures or videos never quite captures the true beauty of them or the overwhelming feeling they create in me. I feel part of the cosmic wonder, the universe. When I share these thoughts and pictures with friends and social media, I'm pretty sure that they're also thinking the same. Aren't we lucky to experience all the nature's wonders and share these experiences?

Travelling makes me happy; life has been kind to hubby and me, though we still have so much more to discover. We love the US, the people, the places, the vast expanses, traditions, just love it. Spain, Poland and India all have their charm and attractions that pull me to them equally for the same reasons. I think most people love travelling and discovering new places, people, cultures: don't you think so?

Cats and dogs make me happy. I think most people love pets. In our early years of marriage, hubby and I thought that we loved dogs and that one day we'd get a dog. While we were both working full time and shifts, it wasn't possible or practical to leave a dog at home all day on his own. You know what I'm going to say here; yes, it all started with a kitten and boy. We became smitten with a kitten.

It all changed when a little kitten walked into our house late one February evening when hubby was playing with the cars in the garage, as men tend to do, leaving the front door wide open. Suddenly, I heard hubby calling me to the small front porch. There was the tiniest of kittens standing there, meowing away. It was around 9pm. We had no idea where it had come from or where we should even look for its owner or mother, as our house was set back from the main road in a lane.

Neither Ian nor I knew anything about looking after cats. I called a work colleague who always had cats. She told us to have a makeshift litter tray and get some kitten food and also make a little bed in a cardboard box until the morning. Hubby went off to the corner shop to get the supplies and the kitten stayed. It did not make any attempt to go anywhere so it stayed in the kitchen for the night.

The next day, we asked around and posted a few cards in the local shops, in case someone was missing a kitten. We tried to give it away to any cat lovers we knew. After a few attempts to get it homed, we decided to keep it. We took it to the vet; had found out by now that he was a boy and so we named him Stucky (pronounced Stooky), after the popular German racing driver Hans Stuck.

Stucky was a gorgeous white cat with tabby patches on him. Stucky loved eating grapes. He tended to pinch the grapes from the fruit bowl, suck away the pulp from the fruit and leave the chewed grapes all over the kitchen floor. We had an even weirder cat than that though, as I will describe shortly.

Hubby decided that now Stucky was part of our family, he needed a pal. I decided that I had to get a matching cat or one that complemented Stucky in his looks so I decided on a black and white cat. I called a few local cat rescue places. One lady answered my call, confirmed that she had a black and white cat, but that it was a runt of the litter so we may not like it. I said I'd go and check it out.

Well, the place was extremely smelly, there were cats everywhere going in and out of the windows. I nearly turned around but thought I'd better just go through with it. You can imagine, can't you? There was no furniture in the place except one chair with torn upholstery. The lady said the cat was in another room so she'd bring him to me, leaving me on my own, standing there in this vile room with torn newspapers shredded, strewn all over the floor. She walked in a minute or so later with this thing that looked like a very big hairy white rat. She let it go and it started darting all over the room, playing with a piece of cardboard that was thrown on the floor.

Apparently, he couldn't meow either; he was a very nervous cat, definitely a runt with hardly any fur on him. There were tufts of hair sticking out all over him. As for the meowing, he made a hissing sound that sounded like 'khe'. I brought him home on a trial. Where I had dreamed of having this beautiful black and white cat, I basically had a big rat in the cat basket.

I asked Ian what I should do as I had no idea how I was going look after it. Hubby just said, "We can't turn our backs on him." I'm sure this sounds familiar to you, if you've ever had cats or dogs as pets. That was that. We called him Rerun after the Peanuts character. Soon enough he and Stucky became buddies; in fact Stucky became Rerun's hero. Rerun followed him everywhere. Rerun was still a scaredy cat, nervous about everything and everyone except me and Stucky.

Stucky and Rerun became inseparable. We'd find them curled up next to the radiator in the sitting room, under the coffee table. Rerun started putting on weight and had nice white fur with little black patches and a black chin. His face was like Felix the cat, used to market the cat food of the same name.

Stucky was a very cool cat – too cool for his own good in the end. One morning he wasn't there when we woke up and we never saw him again. We think he had crossed the busy main road near us just one time too many. We put posters up everywhere and soon had a message from someone who said that they had seen a cat matching his description lying by a waste bin a few days before.

Rerun was pining away for months; we could see that. He wouldn't leave me alone; I became substitute Stucky. Ian decided to get another cat from a local cat shelter and thus started our love affair with cats, as they made their way to our home and our hearts. Every time though we lose one, mainly now through old age (one lived to a ripe old age of 20, something like 140 cat years), it's heartbreaking.

We have become the weird cat-loving people. We love dogs too and as animal lovers often have had to rescue dogs, birds, hedgehogs, rabbits, foxes, deer, just creatures great and small that we come across.

Life is very interesting to say the least when it comes to travelling, children and animals; would you agree with that?

Knowing Yourself

There was a conversation with some friends recently where we were just chatting about our own lives, as we do, and the conversation turned to whether we really know ourselves or acknowledge to ourselves who we are.

I think that a lot of women know themselves and yet for the world, there is a different person showing up. There is the feeling that if I show my true self to myself and to the world, I won't be loved or liked. More to the point, I wouldn't even like myself. This is where it really gets interesting because to me, this is one aspect of ourselves that we have to admit.

I know who I am, and this is the self that has showed up for the last few decades. I have become more tolerant, easier going, as I've got older, perhaps calmer too. To know oneself is also acknowledging what feels right or wrong and that I should follow that feeling through. I've learned to pay attention to my feelings, understanding myself. There are no false pretences.

One of the incidents that sticks out in my mind is that of Mum and the funeral sari. As Mum died so quickly, neither my sister nor I had thought about any of it. We decided that there was a new silk sari that she hadn't worn, one of the heavy ones that she had bought that day in India with all her very expensive ones (mentioned in Chapter 6: Dare to Dream).

It was a dark mink colour with grey tones and gold and silver embroidery work. She had worn all the other gloriously rich silk saris of bright colours, but not this one. Every time Mum took it out of the wardrobe to wear it on a special occasion, she'd put it back and wear something else. It seemed like the right sari for Mum now. My sister and I had to dress Mum at the funeral parlour and just as we were leaving the house, my sister looked at me and said, "No, this is not the right sari."

We both had been feeling that something wasn't as it should be. So now what? This was a Sunday. We didn't have the time to go shopping at the last minute. There was a bright turquoise green silk sari, that had been given to Mum decades ago by one of her brothers, one of our uncles whom she loved and respected very much. She loved that sari.

We laughed amid all that grief at the sheer relief that Mum knew what she wanted and that a dark colour wasn't the right colour for her on her last journey. She'd let us know what she'd wanted. So that's the beautiful sari she wore. Mum was true to herself right to the end. She did not like dark or dull colours, and she was definitely not going to wear one at the end.

What happened to that beautiful new mink-coloured sari, you may well ask. Well, it went back in the wardrobe for another nine years, untouched, in pristine condition because even when I tried to wear it a few times after Mum's funeral, I just didn't feel like wearing it and so it went back into the wardrobe again. It wasn't until my dear friend's daughter was getting married that I knew who that sari had to be gifted to. I gave it to my dear friend's mum who loved it and wore it to my friend's daughter's wedding. It looked absolutely gorgeous on my friend's mum: it was meant for her.

Principles and Standards

We all have principles and standards; we are driven by them. These dictate our character, morals and behaviour. I count myself lucky to have been surrounded by strong women with principles. I find it humbling and yet am very proud that I am part of a dynasty of strong women like my grandma (called *Motibaa*, which means grandma), my aunts, my mum and my cousin sisters, sisters-in-law and nieces. I am also so lucky to be surrounded by people with standards and principles, always learning from all of them.

Just recently, chatting to a friend reminded me of how some of the youngsters are perhaps not as principled as the older generations. In the name of freedom of speech, freedom of behaviour, perhaps letting kids do what they want without any boundaries, sometimes I think doesn't serve them well. It's such a fine line, isn't it?

My grandma and my mum were women of principles and standards. They stood by them. Their life purpose was determined by their standards and principles.

Simple things like daily routines, cleanliness, prayers, charity, feeding others, not only needy people but animals and birds too – everything had to be just so. Mum was very fastidious in her diet and cooking. Their standards of behaviour, giving respect to others was woven into their daily lives.

Both were made of steel but at the same time, so loving.

I remember my grandma never forgot anyone when it came to giving to others, especially to the kids. Grandparents have that role in life, for those of us who are lucky to have them, don't you agree?

Mum and I stayed with my grandma for perhaps a month or more when I was seven.

I remember how she would make sure that I had everything I needed. As a seven-year-old, this was my first experience of India and village life so I was fascinated by everything and everyone. My grandma would explain everything to me patiently, about how things worked, and answer my non-stop questions. She was a great storyteller and her after-dinner stories were always from the scriptures or from her experiences in the village, of our family, my grandfather and our forefathers.

For the duration of our stay with her, she had asked the local tailor to come across with his sewing machine to stitch all of Mum's sari blouses as well as my dresses. He took residence in one of the rooms downstairs in this big house. He would be there from early morning to evening, just sewing.

The material was bought from a couple of textile shops in the village and often my dress was made to match Mum's sari blouse. She always made sure that there was some extra material to make small tote bags and drawstring bags, like small handbags. I used to love grandma's bags that she used to take flowers to the local temple or the feed for the birds by the temple. I wanted all of hers as they were made from various colourful floral print materials. There were lots of green parakeets around the compound of the house: very noisy, but oh such pretty looking birds. They were also fed grain.

Thinking of Mum and principles, an incident in a local grocery shop in Luton in the late 1970s springs to mind. The shop used to deliver at home all the very bulky items that Indians tend to buy, such as large oil drums, bags of rice, bags of flour, lots of different lentils and spices. It was the custom at the time to give the cash to the delivery person, who was one of the people working in the shop. On this particular day, when the delivery arrived, I went to the door, got the items and brought them into the house.

Mum had the money ready in the hallway so I gave the delivery person the money that was due in notes so he could give the change back. However, he couldn't calculate the change we were due so I had to spend some extra time sorting out the maths with him. Mum was listening to all this from the sitting room. Anyway, he gave me the change and left. Some days later, Mum and I visited the shop for more groceries and as we were paying, Mum was asked to pay for the groceries delivered a few days previously.

Mum said that we'd paid. Their records said it was outstanding. Mum said that I had gone to the door and paid, that in fact the delivery guy couldn't add up, so I had to spend time working out the change owed to us.

The shopkeeper insinuated that maybe I had kept the money. Mum couldn't believe what she was hearing. She quietly told him that I didn't need to take the money as it was my money that I had given to Mum from my purse to have it ready for the delivery. Mum asked the shopkeeper to check with the young delivery man what he had done with the money.

She then took some money from her purse, put it on the counter, telling the shopkeeper that she was not going to be humiliated like that and we left the shop without taking any groceries. She did not step into the shop again for nearly a decade, until Mum decided that it was time to forgive and forget. When we did go back, they couldn't do enough for Mum. They knew that they had fouled up big time with Mum. From that day on, we never mentioned the past decade again. Mum was always respected and held in high regard by the owners. The relationship of mutual respect has continued to this day.

What You See is What You Get

Looking back over the past couple of decades, I definitely feel that I can see my mum in me in some of the expressions, mannerisms, thinking, behaviour and even looks. Some flattering, others, ah well, I'm working on them. Mum was very straight-talking, very plain-talking indeed and I feel that as I get older, sometimes, words come out of my mouth not quite as diplomatically as they should.

On the other hand, I feel that there is nothing to hide; what you see is what you get. There are no hidden agendas or facets. Mum was an open book and I feel that I am too. I prefer people to come straight to the point if they have something to say to me, rather than going round the houses.

Life is too short to be anything else. I feel that for serving my life purpose, I have to go with my intuition, my gut feeling, which doesn't happen if I am not totally honest with myself and express myself the way I know. A lot of my nieces and nephews, friends too, have said to me that when I say something to them, it makes sense to them.

I'm happy that they are prepared to listen to me and not only that, take on board what I have said. This can happen only when both parties are totally honest in their communication, with no hidden agendas but respect and love for each other. One of my friends recently asked me where my wisdom came from. How do I know what to say? I said it's the way I am, and if she thought it was wisdom then I was grateful that she thought so.

I have also noticed that in my day-to-day business life, people do listen to me when I say something; often it is nothing to do with the HR service I provide, just about life matters that one discusses in conversations. Quite often now I also get phone calls from business friends to ask my opinion about what's going on in their lives. I truly feel honoured that they value my input.

There have been times – just as happens to all of us in work or relationships with family, friends and colleagues – that despite me being open and honest in my communication, it hasn't been received by the other person in the same vein. In those cases, I have followed Mum's example and advice to let it go. Make your point and withdraw from the conversation, as it's not going to help either of us. Staying true to myself is what matters.

There is no point in having a shouting match or continuing the conversation.

As hubby has often said to me, not everyone is my friend and not everyone is going to love me. Luckily, there have been only a handful of these incidents that mattered enough for me to have been really upset by it.

When it has mattered, what I have found is that every single time, the person has come back into my life at some point and apologised and asked for forgiveness and we've made up.

My simple philosophy is of being true to myself, being honest and open, no compromising on my standards while fulfilling the purpose of my life. My work is done here.

Chapter 10

You Are Much Stronger Than You Give Yourself Credit For

Feel the Fear and Do It Anyway

Life is such a roller coaster and no matter how confident one is about everything in life, sometimes the old doubts creep up or sometimes just a new situation arises to test us.

When Mum was ill, towards the beginning of October, she was getting weaker and sometimes slurring her speech too. It was a tough time to maintain joviality, knowing that we were writing Diwali cards to family in India and friends who had no idea about Mum's health. We were going to write these cards with full of Diwali and New Year cheer, knowing this was the last time that Mum would be signing her name on all these cards, even though she could hardly hold a pen in her hand.

They had to be written all the same, as did my aunt's birthday card for early November; this was for my mum's younger sister, the school principal. This was the same kind of military logistical operation I described earlier – of buying the cards from the Indian grocery shop, writing them, ensuring they were correctly addressed and posted on time. The cards usually bore pictures of our Gods and Goddesses or of divas (the Indian oil lamps in the temples) the latter being more popular these days. Everything is written in auspicious red ink and signed by everyone in the family.

Then the process of addressing them started, making sure that we had the current home addresses. However, in India the postal system actually works very well, and it's amazing how they find the locations of virtually anything when people tend to have 'next to', 'behind' or 'off the main road' as part of the postal address.

Anyway Mum, my sister and I sat around Mum's bed, while she gave instructions on everything, making sure that it was all done the way it had always been done. We did it as though it was just a normal occurrence. My aunt's 70th birthday card was duly signed by everyone with Mum penning a little message of *Aashish* with lots of kisses, xxxxxx, (her blessings, as she always did).

The family told us after Mum's death, and have repeated it to us so many times, how they treasure those last cards they received from Mum. My aunt showed me Mum's card a few years ago when I visited her at her home. She took it out of her cupboard, along with all the other birthday cards that we'd sent her; since Mum's death, I had continued the tradition of doing so. We both were emotional and had a hug and a cry.

All through that last weekend, everything was happening too fast and in some way in slow motion. On the last evening, the Sunday, my sister and I were sure that Mum was going to leave us that night. We took it in turn to stay with Mum, holding her hands, reciting prayers, our Hindu mantras, bhajans and passages from the scriptures. At one point, late at night, Mum's breathing was becoming erratic and so both of us sat on either side of the bed, holding her hands. Mum's feet were very warm, as though all her energy was flowing through them.

We were talking to Mum quietly, telling her that she could go, not to be afraid of anything or worry about anything as everything was fine. She was in good hands; all the dear departed family members were waiting for her. Two nights before this Mum had mentioned that she could see her mother and one of my young cousins, Bipinbhai, who had died a couple of years before, standing there by her bed, smiling as always – and she had also seen one of her sisters-in-law, Bhanu Bhabhi, who had always laughed and joked.

Mum took a deep breath and we thought that this was it, and suddenly all went quiet. She then started breathing normally again. We looked at each other and burst out laughing, crying and laughing at the same time. We had been told in no uncertain terms that she'd go when she was ready; we could hear her saying, "Don't you tell me, I will go in my own time!"

Preparations for the funeral were once again something none of the family had dealt with before; every single thing we did was for the first time and so we had to take a deep breath and just get on with it. Every step of the way, my sister and I had said to Mum, you let us know what you want because we have never had to do this before. Well, you know, she did tell us what she'd wanted all the way through. There were so many little signs of what she'd wanted that we knew she was guiding us. We just held on to that and did what we had to do, the hardest thing in our lives.

Mum died on the morning of Monday, 26 October 2003. We did all we needed to do with the formalities. It was another thing though to call the family in India and give them the news and, for that matter, to tell all our friends and the community. Everyone was just stunned and shocked. There was a torrent of outpouring of grief.

The following two weeks were spent in a robotic trance of getting things done for the funeral. We brought Mum back to Luton as we knew she'd have wanted that. On the day of the funeral, it was sunny and cold. Mum was brought to my house for the last prayers and ceremony. That was tough, but we were supported by the community and friends who were with us all the way through, advising us, taking over arrangements, helping in every way.

We had chosen peachy cream roses for Mum so after the prayers and the rituals, as the funeral directors were taking the coffin to the hearse, I kept thinking, I want one of those roses as a *prasadi*, a memento, but I wasn't going to take any off the large bouquet. As we were closing the house and getting down to the funeral cars waiting for us, strangely there was one single rose on the patio, waiting for me.

As we approached the crematorium, all we could see was a crowd of people waiting in colourful saris and outfits. On a cold November morning, it was so moving to see that people had acknowledged and carried out our request to wear colourful outfits instead of the traditional whites worn at Hindu funerals. The rest of that day was as you can imagine, surreal to say the least, but will stay with us all our lives.

My sister and I had decided to take Mum's ashes back to India as we knew that her heart was in India, with her family and back to her roots. My sister and I flew out in early December and all the arrangements were made with the family so that on the day we landed in Ahmedabad in Gujarat we were going to travel to the holy place of Chanod where the holy river Narmada meets the rivers Orsang and Gupt Saraswati: Triveni Sangam, the meeting of the three holy rivers.

It is a place for *asthi visarjan,* meaning scattering of the ashes. Our aunt, cousin, sister-in-law and my sister and I travelled by car on a four-hour journey to this place, travelled through to the edge of the town and then walked the rest of the way for a few minutes, down a track to get to the river shore. Our cousin brother purchased all the flowers, including lots of roses for the ceremony. Mum loved roses and so had to have lots of them.

It was going to be just us, performing a simple prayer and ceremony. Usually, a priest would perform a ceremony before the ashes are scattered. There were several brightly coloured wooden boats with onboard engines, lined up on the shore. The young men who seemed to be the boat owners were all waiting for customers like us to be ferried to a middle point in the river some ten minutes from where we were to the point where the three rivers met.

One of the young men spoke with my cousin brother and indicated to us to get into this big boat, more like a dhow, for six to eight people. As I neared the boat, I saw it painted in a bright blue colour and thought, Mum's not going to like this boat. Anyway, we all got in it and for some reason the outboard engine wouldn't start. After a few minutes, we were asked to get on to the boat next to it, which was painted in bright red and yellow. I looked up to the sky and smiled. The boat slowly made its way to where the three rivers met and stopped.

The young man asked us to carry out our ceremony. It was a warm day, the water clear, the air quiet with just very muted voices around, a very peaceful and quiet place. On the opposite side of the river, I could see a few people carrying out funeral rites. I still wasn't quite sure if this was the right place, but it was too late by now to change my mind.

As we stopped, I looked up to the shore and there it was, on the cliff, a Lord Shiva temple with its red flag flying away in the still air. That was a good omen. I knew it was the right place. As my sister and I – with the help of our family members – scattered the ashes and then the bagful of flowers, I said to her that I wanted to keep a couple of the roses back as a memento. My sister said, "No – let them all go," so I did that, and let all the flowers go into the clear waters of the three rivers.

As we returned to the shore, I looked down at the boat floor to mind my step as I was about to get off, and lo and behold, there were two small red roses by my feet. I took them, crying and smiling at the same time. I framed each of the roses in identical frames when we returned home to the UK, which my sister and I have in our homes, next to Mum's pictures.

In the Face of Adversity

When faced with adversity, the natural human reaction is of fight or flight. However, at times for me there is yet another way of dealing with those situations – and that is to 'let it be'. Flight is easy and fight can be harmful to both the parties. Letting it be gives a little time to assess the situation and, more importantly, be consciously willing for it to be resolved for both parties.

There's the popular saying, "Sleep on it and you will have an answer." I just let it be and then work at it because that way it always presents me with a workable solution, the one that gives me the opportunity to assess it thoroughly, knowing my limits, my strengths and whether it's going to hurt either party. In the past, I had the tendency either to try dealing with situations there and then, or to worry about them to the nth degree. Neither were really the right approaches for me. I have learned over time what works best for me.

A classic example of this is where someone's being awkward or difficult about a situation that is not going to help either of us. Rather than rushing into it, if it requires for me to let it be, I do, and forget about it. Friends will say, for instance, that they're worrying about a job application they have made or want an answer from a partner or a friend. My advice has been, let it be. It just gets sorted.

I belong to a few networking groups for my business and a couple of these are groups for women. They have been a fantastic support in every way. You find all types of women running all types of businesses. When you start to know one another, there are some amazing stories about why they started their business in the first place. Only recently, speaking with a group of women, there were women running businesses that ranged from art to rent for offices, growing avocados in designer pots and importing beautiful handmade fabrics and artefacts from India, right through to the more 'traditional' businesses of accountancy and law practice.

Often it is because of a career change that has been forced upon the women, or they felt that it was time to do their own thing, or perhaps it is because they now have young children. Have you noticed how diverse and versatile businesses have become? You just have to look at Instagram posts or Google anything you want and there is always someone who has that service or a product as part of their business.

As businesswomen, we are still sometimes hesitant in dealing with adversity because we think we are not good enough or strong enough. However, we always come through. Often it's a case of sharing these issues with one another at the networking forums, getting ideas, assurances, tips for managing them, feeling that confidence of knowing that this has happened to others too and that you're not alone. It's a win for all of us at that point, isn't it? I so love these groups of camaraderie.

There is Always a Way

There is always a way to get things done, have an answer to find a solution. Basically, being open-minded, flexible and quietly determined always shows the way. I love this quote from Steve Jobs, "You can't connect the dots looking forward; you can only connect them looking backwards. So you have to trust that the dots will somehow connect in your future. You have to trust in something – your gut, destiny, life, karma, whatever. This approach has never let me down, and it has made all the difference in my life."

I thought about this a lot when I came across the quote and you know, whether you like Steve Jobs or not, he was right about it. We can only see where we've been by going forward, just doing what we have to do, and the rest takes care of itself.

Only today it happened, and it made me smile through my tears. Today is the 17th anniversary of Mum's death. As it happened in the morning and because I'm up by 5am, the memories flood back as I relive it all once more. I have learned to live with it over the past few years. This morning it was a bit emotional once the messages of love and remembrance from the family started coming in.

I eventually had my shower and sat down in front of my temple for my prayers when I realised that I hadn't bought any Indian sweets for Mum and for the prayers as I usually do for today. Hubby was going to buy the roses for Mum later in the day, so Mum had nothing except the jaggery offered to all the gods and the dear departed during the prayers. Mum preferred savoury and spicy food to sweets anyway.

However, just as I started my prayers, suddenly I stopped because I remembered that I had been given a tiffin box containing steamed Indian spongy rice cakes, a Gujarati speciality called *dhokra*, the day before by one of my 'aunties' in Luton when I visited her to wish her happy birthday. She had made these especially for me as a surprise, knowing that I was going to go across to wish her happy birthday and take her a card and a birthday prezzy.

She had made them freshly once I got to her so I could have some piping hot ones almost as she took them out of the steamer. I also got a packed tiffin of a plastic container with more *dhokras* to eat at home.

Mum loved *dhokra*, we all do in the family. That is one dish that throughout my maternal family has stood the test of time. The recipe is very simple: a thick batter made of rice flour and chickpeas with buttermilk or yogurt and water, whisked together with a little salt and turmeric, left to stand for a couple of hours, add fresh garlic and chillies to taste and just before cooking the batter in small dishes or trays, add baking powder or bicarbonate of soda as a raising agent before placing them in a steamer. You make them spicy by dusting the top with chilli powder or leave them plain.

They take only about ten minutes to cook. Take the tray out, let it cool a little and then cut squares and lift them off gently and serve. Whenever anyone visits, when we go across from the UK to India, we can be sure that *dhokras* will feature somewhere in the menu, often the very first dish that we're offered. I quite often end up having them almost everywhere I visit during the trip. We never tire of them. You eat them steamed with some oil or ghee and often with a fresh garlic and red chilli chutney.

So, coming back to today, there I was for sitting down for my prayers. I quickly got up, warmed up one of the squares of the *dhokras*, added a little fresh oil and offered it to Mum. I was smiling through my tears. It got sorted by Mum. When I told my aunt soon after my prayers what had happened about the *dhokras* that she'd given me yesterday, she was very happy and said that she was blessed. Everything just worked out. Synchronicity, serendipity or what? Don't you just love it?

Another poignant connection to this story is that when Mum died, I had given up eating *dhokra* while Mum was ill. In the Hindu religion, giving up favourite food is like giving up something for Lent in the Christian tradition. Except in this case, it could go on for an indefinite time or for a set period, until your wish has been fulfilled. It's really like a bargaining tool to fulfil your wish.

Here's an example of how this can work – or not. It had been six years since Mum's death when my sister and I had last visited India to scatter her ashes in the sacred rivers. And now I was visiting India again. With three of my cousin sisters, we were visiting Mum's second eldest brother. We sat down for lunch, my Aunt and my Uncle Vinumama, the three sisters and I at the dining table. His daughter-in-law was making hot *dhokra* as family traditions go for a favourite food for the visiting family. It also happened to be our uncle's birthday that day.

I said I wouldn't eat the *dhokras* and would have something else. My sister-in-law said to my uncle, "Binaben is not eating the *dhokras* in the memory of Auntie." My uncle, whom we all loved very much and respected as the patriarch of the family, just looked at me and said quietly with tenderness, "Beta [a term of endearment for a son or daughter], Mummy didn't want you to suffer; don't see it as a punishment of giving up our favourite food, any food. Your mum would want you to be happy, remember her with love every time you eat these, enjoy them and celebrate by knowing how much she loved these *dhokra* as we do."

He didn't say anything else after that. I just started crying. We were all feeling the absence of my mum anyway. No one forced me to eat them. There was such love and feeling in the way he said it, I just asked my sister-in-law to serve me some. I cried all the way through the lunch, but it didn't matter because I was with my family.

So, that episode has stayed in my heart and will carry on so for the rest of my life. It all works out in the end; the dots get joined up for sure.

Chapter 11

When One Door Closes, Another One is Already Open

Trust

I have mentioned before that I have always been looked after in my life by God, the universe, someone up there who has loved me for sure. In my early days of adulthood, I did not have such an awareness or consciousness of being looked after that I now have. Being mindful every time when one door is closing, trusting my destiny of that special future door that has already opened.

A simple example of this is as I mentioned before about career opportunities, something that I had not paid much attention to but looking back, the dots definitely joined up. When I was working for Court Line Aviation, I didn't realise how seriously the company was in trouble. Well, I was a junior in the company and had been there just over a year, so was not up to speed with all the financial details or even the company rumours.

It seemed a good idea to go for the telephonist job at the local telephone exchange and wham, within two-and-a-half months Court Line Aviation had gone into liquidation. Every time that a door was already open for me, I could see the current one closing on me, a chapter of my life coming to an end. It has been the case every time I have had to change my job or career. Recently, over the past few years, I have come to trust the process, which has become the mantra to me.

Several of my friends, family members and business colleagues tend to turn to me for advice or be their sounding board when they have issues with jobs, careers and relationships. They all get the same answer from me, because it means trusting your life with what's going to be the best outcome for you, "Trust the process."

Most recently, someone I have become good friends with through business connections, has an office in the same building as me.

Often he'll walk in, say what he has to say about what's bugging him, kind of letting off steam and walking out expecting me to say the magic words, "Trust the process!" I oblige every time because he knows what to expect. Now it's got to the point where he does have patience and has started to have that awareness of things working out and says, "Yes, I know, trust the process!"

On social media forums, people often tag me on questions asked about contracts of employment, terms and conditions of employment or where the individual feels that they have not been treated fairly. Recently, a young woman called me as she had seen my name mentioned on a forum as an HR consultant who may be able to help. She was in quite an emotional state, as she knew she had been treated badly by her last employer.

We had a half-hour conversation during which I calmed her down, we logically went through all the aspects of her complaint, listed the steps to go back to the employer with her reasoned responses, and outlined her options. I once again made her aware of how perhaps she was still hankering after the closed door of the last employer, being churned up inside by the whole incident, when she should let it go and focus on the door that had already opened up for her.

We also discussed her strengths, her skills and the contribution she could make to an organisation who would appreciate it all. By the end of the conversation, the young woman thanked me profusely, saying she didn't know how to thank me enough for all that I had done for her in that last half an hour. I could feel that she had regained her pride in herself, her sense of self-worth and was ready to walk through that open door with her head held high.

Persevere

A quote by Barack Obama sums it up for me, "Persevere – nothing comes easy. One of the best examples of this is any sport. Many of us are good at something or we just love it because we enjoy the feeling of expression, power, fitness, freedom, good health and generally being just us."

Have you noticed that not all of us are natural sports people? Whatever it is you feel attracted to, you have to work at it. Some of us dedicate our lives to the sports we love because it gives us pleasure and often determines who we are. We come alive, in our own space. It is also understanding our purpose, not being egoistical, but just knowing what works for us. You just give it your all; that one extra push of determination is often what is needed to get us there.

Ian started cycling at the age of 16 when he was in the Army and claims that one of the things that first attracted him to it was that if he joined the camp's cycling club he could leave the base at any time to go training without being challenged. Never mind that he usually ended up in a pub a couple of miles down the road; but that's another story. Thus began his love of cycling long distances and on various terrains on various bikes. At one time he won an Army championship and was offered a professional contract when he returned to Civvy Street. However, in those days, there wasn't any money in it; he had to earn a living and he knew that he really wasn't good enough to turn professional anyway. So cycling became a lifelong passion rather than a career.

Ian has participated in many tough races, for example 20 times in the Three Peaks Cyclo-Cross in the Yorkshire Dales, ten in the Iron Cross Race in Pennsylvania, USA, and several times in the Red Hook Criterium races. What is amazing about him is that he has a realistic view about his ability as a cyclist when it comes to serious racing, so even though he hasn't won any of these races, I admire the fact that he's capable of doing so many of these, time and again, when most of us would not even last a few minutes.

The Red Hook Criterium is a very fast-paced international 'fixed-gear' race series, held on short 1.0–1.5km closed circuits in New York, London, Barcelona and Milan and with no brakes allowed – just don't ask. In all the ones that hubby raced, he was invariably the oldest competitor by a clear margin, with most of the riders being between half or a third of his age. But that didn't stop him from taking part. The race organisers came to know Ian very well and he was always given a great cheer of support when he cycled his laps around the circuit. He just persevered.

Ian has also run a few marathons, including the first London Marathon in April 1981. That was an extraordinary day for everyone who was running, watching or supporting. I'll always remember the fantastic atmosphere as I kind of ran my own marathon in the pouring rain, getting to strategic points in the race before hubby got there. This was such a special race that as they neared the finish line the two leaders, Dick Beardsley and Inge Simonsen, instead of trying to outrun their opponent, stretched out their arms towards each other and crossed the finish line, holding hands, dead-heating as joint winners of the very first London Marathon.

One of the incidents that comes to mind is that of walking down the Eiffel Tower steps on a very cold February day. This is because I don't like walking up or down steps at the best of times, as I mentioned earlier about the stairway in Covent Garden station. Back in February 1985, we decided to have a mini coach trip to Paris; after having had our coach trip to Le Mans in 1984 and having spent one night in the city on the return journey, we wanted to see more. It was on a shoestring budget, and we stayed in a rather run-down hotel in the Montmartre district.

It was OK though for a four-day midweek break because it worked out cheaper that way, and also we were younger and had a higher tolerance of sub-par accommodations than we do now. It was unusually cold and foggy that year, but we did manage to see all the touristy places. It was a case of diving into coffee shops after a couple of hours to get warm or into shops before continuing. I remember using the Métro, which was very reasonable in price.

We of course had to see the Eiffel Tower and luckily, on the day that we chose, it was cold and dry. We didn't have to queue too long to get up to the first level, the main level and then realised that the observation gallery right at the top was also open. Apparently, that was rather unusual, as we discovered afterwards.

So off we went up to the top in a lift, looked at the beautiful views of miles around and being a clear day at the time, it was worth it. We took pictures of all the views, marvelled at the symmetry of the avenues, the buildings and the architecture and were totally enjoying being tourists in one of the world's most beautiful cities.

After being there for about half an hour, we came out to the hallway with the lifts; I think there were two. Well, by this time, there was quite a queue to get down. Hubby didn't want to wait, as we were told that it would be a few minutes before we could take the lift. So, hubby decided that we were going to walk down the steps. I have to confess that I was not at all impressed with the idea. However, hubby was insistent that we did.

We came out of the hallway to the door to the steps, the cold air hitting us straight away. Hubby was already on his way down, so I followed. Now, at this point I have to repeat that I have never liked going down steps, especially if they are the metal grill steps that you sometimes have on railway bridges and through which you can see all the way to the ground below.

Well, these were definitely grill metal steps and we were descending them, going around the main structure, doubly frightening for me. I just took a deep breath and went for it. By the time we got to the main level, my legs were like jelly and I was totally frozen. I looked up to the top of the tower and marvelled at the strength I had found to get down to this level. However, I told hubby in no uncertain terms that he was never going to do that to me again.

So, my dear reader, you know you have the strength and determination in you; you are definitely much stronger than you think. You have to believe in yourself one hundred percent and just go for it – even if sometimes it's not a situation of your own choosing.

Let It Be

The famous Beatles song comes to mind every time I think of Letting It Be, "There will be an answer, let it be…"

It's so difficult to let it be when all you want is the action to get it resolved. It is so very easy to say to someone, "Don't worry, it'll be fine," or "It will turn out all right," or "It'll work out," especially when there are other people involved.

It's a whole different game when it comes to relationships; however, the principle is the same. Let go of that which doesn't serve you, trust the process and move on because there is someone better waiting for you. It may take a little longer than you expected, but it will happen. Just let it be.

Auntie Bina has had many of these conversations with family members, friends and sometimes just acquaintances who tend to want to confide in me, want my opinion, some have even said my wisdom, I hasten to add, both men and women. This is just like being a psychiatrist, mentor, aunt, life coach, all rolled into one. I am grateful that people want to share their worries, their innermost thoughts and feelings, their heartaches with me.

Most times the person knows the answer; it's just that they want a second opinion or someone like me to listen to them because they know that I will at least empathise with them. However, I will also give them my honest perspective. Many a time, there have been tears, long conversations about options, the future, their current state, why they can't let go and don't want to let go.

There is also that feeling of false hope that if they ignore it, it will sort itself out. To me, letting it be is not the same as ignoring it. It's all about the answer coming from the heart when you purposely leave it alone for a while and the answers present themselves. Often, it is also a case of being open-minded, allowing opportunities to present themselves to us and for us to consider every one of them. Have you noticed how opportunities often turn up from the weirdest of connections or places?

A friend had been made redundant last year from a company and despite looking for suitable work, she couldn't find what she wanted. She is very creative and has always had a hobby of making things, knitting, baking and making ornaments; she also likes everything to do with energy, crystals and meditation. Suddenly she found the answer in supplying directly to like-minded people and to larger shops through Instagram and other online retail platforms.

I know a few women who, having had corporate careers in their 20s and 30s, decided that they wanted something more out of life, and turned to their life interest of yoga and meditation. One of my lovely cousins, having had a great career in the financial world, on retirement trained as a yoga master. She's not only loving it for herself, but changing so many lives around her.

Expectation

This is the time of expecting the best for yourself. Not looking back or having any doubts about your destiny. I know you may say that in the circumstances in which you have found yourself, "This is so far-fetched, Bina, that it doesn't relate to me." My take on it is, "What have you got to lose? You may end up with what you think you possibly should, or perhaps – taking on board what I am suggesting – you may just find something much better."

I read something this morning from the book *The Secret* that made me smile, "Remember to remember, the messages are all around you. Remember to be aware, be present in the moment." I love it because it's such a great aspect of being in the moment. It's a way of training your mind to tune in to what's happening around us in the universe – and when we become aware of these signs, it's amazing how they tend to lead to what we want.

I remember that being aware is when coincidences start happening: synchronicity and serendipity at their best.

In recent years, more and more coincidences are happening. I put these down to the fact that my expectation of things that will happen for me has gone up. It's everything coming together to make it a certainty.

The coincidences are also where so many times friends have remarked how they were thinking of me and I'd call them or message them. It's all such good fun. I would like you to try it. Expect with all your heart and conviction a best outcome for you every time you want something. Then just let it be. It happens.

Here's something that will make you smile. I had not thought about the title of the book and my coach, Mindy, had said, "We won't worry about it until you are ready to prepare the second draft." During one of my sessions with Mindy, I happened to say something like, "There is a common thread running through our stories," and suddenly Mindy said, "Thread, I like that!"

She then pointed to the red thread I have tied around my right wrist, "You mean the *rakhi*?" and I replied, "No, I wasn't thinking of that." We left that conversation there about the thread, which was a long time ago, in the early stages of writing this book. So when we started thinking of a title, Mindy asked me if I had thought of anything for the title and the only thing I could think of was something to do with threads or thread. After a long while, having tried out different adjectives and permutations of phrases with the word thread, such as invisible, loving and eternal, in the end, I just looked up towards the ceiling as I sat in my Zoom meeting with Mindy and said, "I'll ask Mum, she'll sort it out." I also told Mindy that I would sleep on it. I had to let it be.

In the evening, as I was playing with words to go with thread, a definition of 'the red thread of fate' jumped up at me on Google and I said, OMG, OMG as it said that the thread may stretch or tangle but it will never break. People who are destined to meet are tied together with an invisible thread.

The red thread that Mindy had referred to such a long time ago suddenly came to life. The whole book is based on different people who have been part of my world. We came full circle back to *The Red Thread*.

I Am Special

Have you noticed how kids, even toddlers or young children, are so sure of themselves? They have no inhibitions. They don't have any reservations about their capabilities or their expectations of what they want. They just zoom in to what they want with that certainty that it's theirs.

Well, we have such a lot to learn from them. I had forgotten about myself over the years as being a very important person, a special person in my life, while tending to others' needs and wants, even wanting to think about others before myself. I am now changing my priorities a bit at a time. I am special and I am important is the mantra we have all seen in so many self-help books and articles. To read it is one thing, to practise it is a totally different way of living.

What does it really mean and how have I incorporated it in my life? When you feel that others are more important in your life than you, others' needs have to be tended to before yours or you don't even pay attention to your own needs, then it's definitely time to review it. Thinking of others doesn't stop us from having our own needs fulfilled.

A simple example is how most women have to plan for looking after the family's needs and wants. One of the simplest things that can be changed in that scenario is for the woman in the Asian household to sit down for dinner with the family.

What happens a lot when I'm in India is that my sisters-in-law always ask me to sit down with the elders for lunch or dinner, while they have their meal afterwards. Even when I recently visited a younger cousin sister, she indicated that she'd have the meal after everyone else had eaten.

There is the tradition of serving hot rotis and hot food to the family, so in a way it defeats the objective of everyone eating together. It often then ends up with the sister-in-law running around serving hot food to everyone while she's eating her dinner. I do the same when I'm entertaining, and I get into serving mode. Can't win sometimes on this one.

I do make time for myself, no matter what. It's once again a discipline of not forgetting the fact that I'm going to make time for myself in my day.

One of the other things that has happened over the last few years is that as I have focused a lot more on my likes more than dislikes, it's changed my outlook on life. It has started to bring in more positive results. These are simple steps of training the mind not to say 'no' as an instinct or as a reflex action. It is also about remembering that I am special and so it's all working out for me, all in the right way, in the right timeline.

My involvement in the local Indian community has increased, and in general I am able to spend more time listening to Indian music and classical music, sharing video clips and music clips with like-minded family members and friends. This may not seem a big deal to others, but it means a lot to me as in the past I'd have thought to myself that I didn't have the time for it. Now I make time for it because it matters to me and I love it.

So, my dear reader, my simple message to you is that you should make time for the things you love, to be with the people you love; life is for living and each of us matter. YOU are special, I am special, WE are special.

Chapter 12

Everything Works Out in the End

Fun Times

One thing we all have in common is that we all love celebrations, being with people with whom we can share laughs, good food, drinks and have a good time. It doesn't matter at all whether or not we have to have a special reason other than being together. I love both organised and impromptu occasions.

In Kampala, we used to have get-togethers almost every weekend with my father's side of the family – my father's eldest brother and his family. We all got on very well as a big family and there were usually also several other friends and their families there. This was all centred around the men taking the lead in arranging these get-togethers. The women, including Mum, my aunt, sister-in-law and older cousin sisters disappeared in the kitchen for hours to make the food. There would have been at least 20 or more people each time, all with large appetites, so the meals were cooked in large quantities.

Given that it was Gujarati food, especially if it was some religious celebration or just because we were all together, there would be Indian sweets, savoury dishes – rice, roti or puris (puffed fried round wheat Indian flat bread), at least one green vegetable, one bean or lentil-based dish called either *kathol* (bean) or *daal* (lentil soup). There would be accompaniments of salad, chutneys, pickles, poppadum, yogurt or buttermilk, followed by ice cream and fruit. The kids and men would be the first to have their lunch, all sitting on the floor, with the meal served in huge stainless steel plates. You have probably seen them, because nowadays thalis appear on the menu of nearly every Indian restaurant in the UK. Thali means a plate.

The fun thing about these was the loud conversations between the men daring each other on a bet as to who could eat the most.

Brahmins love sweets and Indian sweets tend to be very heavy, mainly made with ghee, wheat or chickpea flour and lots and lots of sugar. There are milk-based sweets too, which don't have ghee or flour in them, and tend to be more like milk puddings or yogurt-based *shrikhand*, all flavoured with saffron, nutmeg, cinnamon, cardamom and garnished with lots of nuts, such as cashews, pistachios and almonds.

Well, going back to the dares, it was normal for the men to eat lots of sweets. One of the popular sweets was *laddoos* – sweet balls made of wheat flour, ghee and jaggery (sugar cane unrefined sugar) with nutmeg in them. Normally one is enough for anyone. My father, cousins and uncle could easily eat up to ten, no problem. Even I, at five or six, could easily eat three. I loved sugar cane jaggery so much that from the time I was perhaps two or three, when I woke up in the morning, the first thing I would do after brushing my teeth, would be to go to the larder in the kitchen, sit on the floor, point at the big jar of jaggery and insist on a lump of it for breakfast. I had to have some every day.

Then there were the picnics at the botanical gardens of Entebbe. The distance from Kampala to Entebbe is around 23 miles. In my childhood days, when cars were not that common in Kampala, we used to pile up in a minibus or a couple of cars and when I say pile up, I mean pile up. It was not a problem to get eight or nine of us in a small family saloon car. Once I remember that a cousin hired a flatbed truck and we all piled up in the back. It was a warm day, so we made a makeshift sail like an awning from a gunnysack hessian cloth to give us some shade from the midday sun.

The attraction of the picnic was always about having a simple lunch that was cooked by the men over a charcoal fire or on paraffin stoves. It was a mixed vegetable curry, rice and moong split peas made into a *khichadi*, wheat crispy *bhakhris* and yogurt and pickles.

The vegetable dish was a family speciality of an *undhiya*, a mixed vegetable curry with dumplings, with lots of freshly roasted spices such as cinnamon and cloves stirred in it. The family had given this dish the name of *bogho*, a derivation of the Swahili word *mboga*, meaning vegetables. The lunch was always amazing, and I can still smell the spicy delicious food.

The mixed vegetable curry was cooked by the men while the women made tons of the *bhakhris* (crispy rotis) and *khichadi*. I must add here that all the men in the family were excellent cooks. The kids went adventuring among the cocoa plants, the coffee beans and the lush tropical greenery, working out the names of the plants. After the lunch, everyone played games and then it was time to visit the shore of Lake Victoria and dip our toes in the water. The homeward-bound journey was in the early evening before sundown.

The picnics I remember fondly here in the UK have been either in the garden or at Dunstable Downs with Mum, overlooking the London Gliding Club. The vistas are beautiful from the downs. In the early days, we used to get a bus to the downs, with our Indian packed lunch of parathas, potato *shaak* and often cheese sandwiches, bhajis and something sweet like biscuits or Jaffa cakes: a mixed menu. It can be very windy on the downs due to its altitude, but we all loved the place. It didn't matter if it was windy; we had our picnic.

In later years, I used to drive Mum up there on a Sunday, park, buy the 99p ice cream cones with a Cadbury flake in each of them from the ice cream van and just watch the world go by. It was lovely in the summer months, seeing the kites being flown by people, the gliders taking off and landing far below us and families generally having a great time.

My love of flying kites or watching kites being flown is childlike, I'll freely admit. In my younger days, I flew them not only in

Ahmedabad, at the city's kite-flying festival of Sankrant on 14 January – but also many years later in freezing temperatures at Dunstable Downs, just because it happened to be 14 January and the Gujarati kite-flying festival day.

Mum loved entertaining and so often it was for a committee meeting for the Luton Brahmin Association or just getting a few people to come over for lunch or dinner. On these occasions Mum had invariably been hard at work cooking from early morning until it was all done. She was an excellent cook, as I have mentioned before, and it was always an elaborate meal, never a one-dish meal. All our family members and friends still remember Mum's cooking with fondness.

Around this time, something odd started to happen when Mum was cooking. Often, as she was about to serve the meal or sometimes even halfway through, food would just slip from her hands and fall on the floor. Sometimes, it would even be raw ingredients that she was just about to start cooking with or sometimes she would be opening a packet of biscuits and one would fall on the floor, as if moved by an unseen hand. She was getting thoroughly fed up with it all, so she finally decided that it was someone, something – or some of the dear departed souls – who wanted it, especially if it was something very tasty. From then on, whenever it happened Mum would tell them aloud, "You just wait; I'll serve you when the meal is ready, have some patience!" In addition, from then on at every mealtime, a separate plate was made up for 'them', a tradition that I have continued in my own way.

To this day, both my sister and I do the same thing, especially during religious festivals, birthdays or special occasions. But it happens to me a lot anyway when I am cooking or about to take some Indian ready-made snacks out of a packet or container. Something will fall on the floor, so I always have the plates and bowls ready for 'their' food and snacks. Nevertheless, I do question the reason why 'they' would want to eat a piece of raw onion or potato – but hey, who am I to question it?

When Mum was ill, a cousin had come to the UK on business and was going to pop in to see us. By this time, we had the diagnosis and Mum had started to feel the tiredness. She wanted to cook the meal for him and she made a full Gujarati celebration meal for him and for all of us. We did not let on to him about Mum's health. That was the last time she ever cooked. It was a good time, an emotional time, but a good time.

Fun times with families in India have always been centred around food and music, whether on the terrace of the family's apartment building, or a day out to a temple. It's always about family, friends, food, music and sharing precious moments and laughs.

Ian and I love travelling. So often when exploring in any country, we'll have some food and drink with us, stop at some picnic spot and just watch the world and the traffic go by. Impromptu picnic.

When it comes to our friends in Poland, Spain and the US, once again, sharing food, music, good conversations and generally having a laugh has been the aim, making memories, even in the coldest of winters or most burning hot summers, these have been the best times and I know that they will continue.

Evolving

I love this quote by Maya Angelou, "I have created myself, I have taught myself so much".

We all evolve; it's a fact of life. Sometimes it's unconscious evolution, sometimes it's conscious evolution. The events in our life mould us, we mould ourselves to who we want to be, who we aspire to be.

In all of this, we learn so much.

When Mum was 15, she was educated to the matric standard, finishing school before she was married and emigrated to Uganda. For a naïve, young girl who had led a sheltered life, here she was travelling thousands of miles to another continent. All through her life she taught herself new things, used her education to teach boys at school who were older than her, taught herself to cook, sew and knit, learned to be a housewife and a mother of two girls, and then came to the UK as a refugee.

She didn't stop evolving because she went off to work and learned the new ways of this country, to live within different communities and become a person of gravitas, compassion, genuine interest in others and one that was loved and respected as an elder in the community. Mum also found happiness in her later years through being part of her greater family and the community and having the freedom to be herself.

My personal growth has been in a similar fashion, not a straight line of achievements or targets, as you will know by now simply by having read this book. Nevertheless, I feel that I have done all right so far, however circuitous my path may have been, from a sheltered life in Kampala to where I am now, running my own business in the UK. Life is what you make of it and to be honest, yes, it could have been a lot better but 'it is what it is', as they say, and I feel proud that I have evolved to be a balanced person.

I have evolved to be a businessperson, which I would have never imagined in a million years. I have been so lucky with every step of my career, learning all the time. I have been equally lucky in being surrounded by people far more intelligent and smarter than I to whom I could turn to when I got stuck.

Then there's the part of me which has evolved naturally, or perhaps I have inherited it from my mum, the knack of being there for others as an adviser, an aunt to anyone who has needed to offload or wanted someone to listen to them. Someone they could trust with their innermost thoughts, anxieties and fears. Someone who would give them practical advice and be totally honest every time.

Learning has become part and parcel of life, and to be honest, I'm no different from anyone else. All of us are learning something new every day, from just watching social media clips or reading a book or Googling. What on earth did we do before Google? It has become such an integral part of our lives. Dictionaries, reference books, paper maps – they are all almost completely defunct now.

Well, the process of evolving will carry on till the end. I cannot see myself ever stopping learning. I'm too inquisitive and much too nosy. I always need to know.

I Owe to a Lot of People

None of us live in isolation. Not even someone who has decided to forsake the world completely and gone off to become a sage or a hermit. They would still have had some people around them to help them make those decisions – in both positive and negative ways.

I owe a lot to many people in my life for helping me to become who I am, what I am. The ones who loved me and even those who for whatever reasons ultimately didn't.

I owe to my mum, and even my father, for instilling the high moral values in me; to my sister and family, my paternal and maternal families, my hubby and every person I have met who has contributed to my life.

I owe to all those who gave me an opportunity each time in my career, from the manager who gave me my first job to the ones who helped me, coached me and mentored me to progress every step of the way. I owe it to all those colleagues who worked with me, offered camaraderie and companionship, and were patient with me; and those who encouraged me to do better and all those who worked in my teams as part of my life. I owe it to my former business partner to jointly start our HR consultancy.

I owe to all those who encouraged me to turn a dream of writing this book into a reality.

I owe to all those who have walked into my life and have accepted me as I am, have become my friends and part of my extended family, loved me, cherished me and supported me; you all know who you are.

I owe to my Hindu community friends in Luton, the Indian community, the town communities, the business community at large, my clients who again have accepted me for who I am and have become very much part of my life and let me into their world of business, being part of their teams.

I owe to every single person who has made me laugh, be happy and feel special in every way. I owe to those who don't even know me, but whose life stories have touched me; their principles have made me review mine, made me stronger. I owe to those who inspire me every day: strong women who have become role models such as Michelle Obama, Kamala Harris and many others in everyday life.

I owe to a whole lot of people, but most of all, to my Mum. So I love you all and thank you.

The Book

I am nearly at the end of writing this book. It has been a long journey. Now that I am here, it feels strange that I will have no more chapters to write after this one. As I pointed out at the beginning of this book journey, this book has been in the making for the last ten years at least.

I am not a writer and never thought I would ever be one. After Mum's death, writing a book became a burning desire for me. I wanted to write her story; there were so many lessons in her life that I wanted people to know about, about her strength, her principles, her love. I interviewed several family members, especially my aunts and uncles, over the past ten years, recording their conversations with me, making notes of everything they said about Mum.

All the same, each time, there was something that stopped me going further with actually writing the book. A couple of years ago, through a business associate, I met Mindy, who I learned helped individuals to write books – a book writing coach as it were. I thought about our meeting, but did nothing about it and again another year went by. Nonetheless the desire was still strong in me to write the book.

Months passed while I pondered, and then I contacted Mindy once again. It was clear straight away that it was meant to be this time, because everything fell in place over a day and a 30-minute conversation. The time was right; it was the right time for it to be written.

This book is not just a book, it's about life journeys, entwined and held together with invisible threads. It's my effort to demonstrate to you, my dear reader, that it does not matter how dark life may seem at times, where you may be in your life journey – you matter, you are strong, you will always come though. You have that ability to hang on in there, to keep remembering every moment of your life that you are special, and the world is a wonderful place because you and I are in it.

It's Definitely Not the End. xx

About the Author

My life began in Uganda, born to Indian parents. We were a small family, made up of my sister and me and our mum and dad. We enjoyed our life in the tropics, full of family, community and education. It was a life of values, ethics and standards. However, family life was of two halves; what happened in the home was not what was portrayed to the outside world.

In early August 1972, the president of Uganda, Idi Amin, ordered the expulsion of the country's Asian population, giving them 90 days to leave. This was terrifying, and we had to go. We left for the UK, arriving in Luton on 7 October 1972, a day I will never forget. We were lucky, as we all spoke English. My mother spoke excellent English, having been a teacher in Entebbe. This made the transition to life in the UK easier, but we had to adapt to British weather.

Not long after we arrived, my father left us and went back to India, leaving my mum to raise my sister and me. We carved out a life for the three of us with determination to make it a success.

After being in the country for six weeks, I started a job as a junior data clerk in a company called Court Line Aviation at Luton Airport. After about 18 months in the company, I started my career in telecommunications and IT with BT and, over the years, worked my way up, educating myself to move towards a job in HR. This led me to my role in HR and a long career at London Luton Airport. In 1981 I married Ian, a wonderful man with whom I share an amazing love of life and travel. Sadly in 2003 my beloved mum died, and she would be so thrilled to know this book has been written.

In 2009, I left the airport and started my own business, Plain Talking HR, initially with a business colleague, Bronwen Philpott. We enjoyed building the business together and carved an excellent reputation in Luton. Our specialism was working with small and medium-sized companies to support them with all aspects of their HR. Having worked together at Luton Airport, we knew each other well. We knew our partnership would drive the business forward. When we started the business, there were very few HR consultancy practices, especially in the Luton area. The business proved to be successful. Bronwen retired a few years ago, and I have continued to build on the work we did and to grow the business.

My passion is inspiring other women – particularly Asian women and older women – to start and grow sustainable businesses. Having started my business when I was 57, much later than most entrepreneurs, I feel that my story proves you are never too old to start a business.

I help with as many community projects as I can, including being a Governor at Luton Sixth Form College, Trustee of Level Trust,

Sixth Form Employers' Advisory Board. Student Mentor sponsored internships. I also support the Navaratri Association, Luton Brahmin Association of Luton and the local Hindu temple. Being a volunteer is very rewarding and I encourage anyone to get involved in local charities and projects. We should all make an effort to give back as much as we can to support others.

Gender equality is important to me, so I am part of the steering group for Bedfordshire & Luton Community Foundation (BLCF). Their initiative is called Evolve for gender equality and I regularly advise on employment and HR law matters.

Work continues to be important to me and is a big focus in my life. Plain Talking HR is flourishing. In 2021, I was selected as one of the top 100 female entrepreneurs in the *f:*entrepreneur #ialso campaign. I have also been chosen as a finalist in many local and national awards, including SME Bedfordshire Awards, The National Paralegal Awards and The Best Businesswomen Awards.

With family spread across the globe, I spend a lot of my free time visiting relatives and friends, but I am always happy to come home and spend time with my much-loved feline family. Retirement is certainly not on the agenda.